CW00515782

Plant-Based Meal Plan Cookbook

The Ultimate 28-Day Vegan Meal Plan for Weight Loss, How to Reset Metabolism and Cleanse your Body with Whole Foods Recipes for Beginners and Busy People.

[Thomas Slow]

Legal & Disclaimer

The information contained in this book and its contents is not designed to replace or take the place of any form of medical or professional advice; and is not meant to replace the need for independent medical, financial, legal or other professional advice or services, as may be required. The content and information in this book has been provided for educational and entertainment purposes only.

The content and information contained in this book has been compiled from sources deemed reliable, and it is accurate to the best of the Author's knowledge, information and belief. However the Author cannot guarantee its accuracy and validity and canno be held liable for any errors and/or omissions. Further, changes are periodically made to this book as and when needed. Where appropriate and/or necessary, you must consult a professional (including but not limited to your doctor, attorney, financial advisor or such other professional advisor) before using any of the suggested remedies, techniques, or information in this book.

Upon using the contents and information contained in this book you agree to hold harmless the Author from and against any damages, costs, and expenses, including any legal fees potentiall resulting from the application of any of the information provided by this book. This disclaimer applies to any loss, damages or injury caused by the use and application, whether directly or

Table of Contents

5

INTRODUCTION

Why I wrote this book

There are so many things to know about the plant-based Diet, a real lifestyle that involves not only the choices at the table but also essential implications on what you decide. Here is a guide on how to make it your lifestyle.

Proper and balanced plant-based Diet: how to do it?

Find plant-based diet specialist or remote nutritional consultancy service created to satisfy the need and is aimed at everyone, with particular attention to pediatric patients, pregnant women and the elderly.

In any case, however, it is not necessary to consult a nutritionist simply for wanting to switch to a plant-based diet; it becomes so when you have specific needs. To stay healthy, on the other hand, is essential to follow a varied and balanced diet.

Why you should read this book

This intuitive and easy-to-read book is a complete guide for beginners to help you get started a Plant-based diet without stress.

Based on studies, one of the most effective ways you can boost your energy levels, prevent chronic diseases, and improve your health is to start a plant-based diet. Changing one's nutrition is considered to be an effective way to live longer and reduce the risk of falling sick. If you are interested in getting the most important information about a Plant-based diet, here is the book you are looking for.

Protein intake is the main concern of many who want to switch to a plant-based diet. Therefore, we provided all the necessary facts about the Plant-based diet in general and, in particular, about protein intake. Learn how to easily switch from an animal diet to healthier plant-based food without sacrificing delicious foods.

We will share with you simple and easy steps on how to start a Plant-based diet without harm to your health. And these simple steps will help you to achieve your goal!

Plant-based Diet and sport: is it possible (even at high levels)?

Not only is it possible, but even advisable. In recent years, more and more sporting, even at the highest levels, have chosen to exclude meat and animal products from their Diet, maintaining excellent results or even increasing them. To prove it, not only the numerous plant-based diet athletes at the Olympics but also the scientific evidence: be it amateur or professional - is not only advisable but even beneficial. For those who practice physical activity, a diet that guarantees energy is important necessary for training, but also integrating the mineral salts and vitamins that will inevitably be lost during physical exertion, as well as the fundamental proteins for muscle recovery.

Plant-based Diet and children NO danger to health

Many myths gravitate around the plant-based Diet, but the most widespread is that according to which it would be a difficult diet to follow, rigid and not suitable for children. Again, however, experts tell a different truth. The plant-based Diet is not only suitable for children, but it is also healthier compared to other types of diets. The most obvious benefits are mentioned by the American Academy of Pediatrics and concern the rarity of overweight and lower blood cholesterol levels in plant-based die children. But in general, all international guidelines classify plant diets as healthy, even in children. However, if a child is fed an adequate and balanced plant-based diet, not only will he not face deficiencies, but will find numerous health benefits.

No danger even for plant-based Diet during pregnancy, on the contrary: this is a preferred choice, even for omnivorous women. This is because, as the expert explains, plant-based Diet is the one that exposes the fetus to fewer risks, such as endocrine disruptors or environmental pollutants. This, however, is not enough: the plant-based Diet is suitable for any age, even in the elderly. The advantages of this food choice in old age, among which the possibility to effectively prevent and treat chronic diseases such as diabetes, cardiovascular diseases, obesity and overweight stand out.

What do plant-based diet individuals eat?

Once you've discovered that plant-based Diet is advisable at every stage of life, it's time to find out what to bring to the table! First, it may be useful to draw up a plant-based diet shopping list, trying to understand how and with which foods plant-based diet individuals replace traditional ones. It is also important to check the labels, which often hide ingredients of animal origin hidden behind unclear alphanumeric abbreviations.

Understanding what plant-based diet individuals eat is quite simple, in reality: fruit, vegetables, oilseeds, and dried fruit form the basis of a 100% plant-based diet, to which foods can also be added (completely optional) like seitan, tofu, tempeh and the like. The plant-based Diet, therefore, is not only suitable for everyone and at any age, but it is also a collection of foods, flavors, and tastes that are often new and original, a must try!

A brief overlook of the contents

A plant-based diet is all about celebrating and enjoying the foods that naturally fuel our bodies and are minimally processed. By improving your nutrition, you can improve your health, which is exactly what the plant-based diet is about. Don't dramatically change your diet without consulting your doctor to make sure that here will be no medical issues, such as problems with medications you may currently be on. You should also gradually change to the plant-based diet if you are a heavy meat eater.

It's that simple and I like to keep things that way. Yet not every plant-based diet is the same. You can make it **your** lifestyle and adjust it as you see fit.

There are a few lifestyle changes one needs to do to start a plant-based diet. Going in too strongly will cause tension to build up only to be blown when a craving hits. Some may find it very difficult to follow but you only need to keep a few points in mind to achieve success.

Increase greens in your diet. A variety of vegetables are present for choosing to offer different flavors and textures for soothing your tongue. Pick vegetables regularly for meal bases and a replacement for unhealthy snacks. The crunchiness and flavors of some veggies might decrease the likelihood of eating junk food.

Most healthy diets don't just forbid the consumption of fats but instead tells you to replace bad fats which are derived from animals with good ones derived from plants. Seeds and olive oil are a good source of healthy fats which do not increase the body cholesterol levels.

Cut down meat, especially red meat as much as you can. You can still consume it if you are following a more lenient diet but it is discouraged. Replace your meat with seafood or tofu which can be a good substitute for it.

Rather than putting desserts on the table, you should place fruits or fruit dishes. They are a healthier option with the same hints of sugar to satisfy the sweet tooth. Some people crave sugar more, they can slowly cut off sugar from their diet by switching it for sweet fruits instead.

Replace everyday cow's milk for plant-derived milk such as soy, almond, rice or coconut. Milk is an important part of a diet that is impractical to fully remove from the diet.

Stay away from foods that have a lot of sugar like a Pepsi or are high in fat like french fries. Also do not buy processed food because they are riddled with salt and sugar, hich are enemies to your body.

Be aware that not every nutrient is being provided fully and arrange a replacement for that. Vit B12 is present in some cereal and in nutritional yeast. Iron is also less consumed so eat a healthy dose of cabbage, spinach or kidney beans to make up for it.

Chapter 1: The Plant-Based Diet

The history of Plant Based Diet

As you can imagine, humans have been consuming a plant-based diet before the invention of McDonald's and some of our other favourite fast-food chains. To begin our journey, I am going to start us off in the times of the hunter-gatherer. While we could go back even further (think Ancient Egypt!), I believe this is where a plant-based diet becomes most relevant.

Hunting and Gathering

The hunter-gatherer time period is where we find the earliest evidence of hunting. While we do have a long history of eating meat, this was a point in time where consuming meat was very limited. Of course, humans eating meat does not mean we were carnivores; in fact, the way we are built tells us differently. Yes, we can consume meat, but humans are considered omnivores. You can tell this from our jaw design, running speeds, alimentary tract, and the fact we don't have claws attached to our fingers. History also tells us we are omnivores by nature; however, the volution of our human brains led us to become hunters so that we could survive.

The need for hunting did not come around until our ancestors left tropical regions. Other locations influenced the availability of plant-based foods. Instead of enduring winter with limited amounts of food, we had to adapt! Of course, out of hunger, animal-flesh becomes much more appealing. This early in time, our ancestors did not have a grocery store to just pop in and buy whatever they needed. Instead, they used the opportunity of hunting and gathering to keep themselves alive.

Agriculture

Eventually, we moved away from hunting and gathering and started to become farmers! While this timeline is a bit tricky and agricultural history began at different points in different parts of the world, all that matters is that at some point; animals started to become domesticated and dairy, eggs, and meat all became readily available. Once this started, humans no longer needed to hunt nor gather because the farmers provided everything we could desire!

Principles of a Plant Based Diet

You can eat:

All vegetables, including greens like spinach, kale, chards, collards, asparagus, broccoli, cauliflower, bell peppers, tomatoes, onion, etc

All fruits, including berries, avocado, apple, banana, watermelon, grapes, oranges, etc

Plant-based alternates to meat like tofu and tempeh

Plant-based milk and dairy products including coconut milk, almond milk, peanut butter, almond butter, cashew yogurt, etc

All whole-grains, including brown rice, amaranth, quinoa, barley all beans, whole wheat pasta, whole-grain bread, etc

All nuts, including cashews, almonds, walnuts, macadamia nuts, etc

All seeds like chia seeds, flaxseed, hempseeds, etc

Lentils

Millets

Flax eggs

Honey, maple syrup, coconut sugar, stevia, Splenda, erythritol, etc

Unsweetened coffee and tea

You can not eat:

- Meat including beef, pork, and poultry
- Seafood including fish and shrimps
- Processed animal products like hot dogs, sausages
- Dairy items like butter, eggs, whole milk, yogurt, etc
- Sweetened drinks like soda, fruit juices, sweetened tea and coffee
- Fried food and fast foods
- White bread and white pasta

Plant Based Diet vs Vegan Diet

When we commonly hear about the plant-based diet the only thing that comes to our mind is being vegetarian or vegan. It is a kind of reflex in our minds that lets us connect the links to the information that we already know. In order to specify the real functions of the plant-based and vegan diet, it is necessary to know the difference between both. Most people confuse the two and consider them the same. These two are not same but like each other. In this chapter, you will get to know about some of the interesting facts about vegetarianism and focusing on a plant-based diet.

Understanding veganism

Before proceeding any longer, you need to know what vegetarianism, veganism or vegan diet is. Vegan or vegetarian is a specific group or community of the people who ethically, religiously and on cultural basis avoid using all meat products in any manner. They not only quit using the animal passed food products but also all kinds of animal products such as leather, eggs, milk, honey and more. They believe in an animal-friendly environment and consider using animal products or eating meat as an act of cruelty.

Following their beliefs and instincts, they make sure to avoid every possible thing that is directly or indirectly in link with animals. The vegan food or diet is all about plant-based options that do not contain any contents of animal products. They consume everything randomly that includes the processed food options, artificial sugar and other baked or canned food options from the vegetables and beans.

16

The goal of the vegan diet is to exclude the animal products and animal-based diet/food from the regular diet. They want to keep the animal secure and do not want to harm their lives and the whole mechanism. According to them, they take the initiative to help animals live a peaceful and happy life in the community. Vegan diet has nothing to do with a motive of healthy living.

A fine line differences

Most people have confusion in understanding a vegan diet and a plant-based diet. If we have a close look at the vegan diet or being vegetarian, then it states that one should eat all the vegetables and avoid any meat products. It is simply that a person prefers eating vegetables and fruits instead of meat and other fats. However, note that the vegan diet is a part of the vegan culture that involves not using any other animal products, not in food nor any daily use.

On the other hand, a plant-based diet is all about easy healthy plant food option that includes fruits, vegetables, lentils, beans and more. Other than the hardcore plant diet options, it allows the intake of low-fat dairy products that include low-fat milk, low-fat cottage, mozzarella and cheddar cheese as well. Having a plant-based diet doesn't require that you avoid all the animal-based products.

Identifying the difference

It is necessary for everyone to identify the basic difference between the vegan diet and a plant-based diet. Veganism is a par of the culture and belongs to a specific community while a plant-based diet is a simple diet procedure that helps anyone to eat healthy and fresh.

Difference in approach

The major difference between the plant-based diet and a vegan diet is the basic approach. People adopt a plant-based diet to move towards a healthy and refreshing lifestyle. They want to exclude all the toxins from their life and body. While on the other hand, the vegan diet is all about showing love and support for animals by avoiding all the animal products and eating vegetarian food.

How do you start a Plant Based Diet

It's is not easy to make a change in any diet that you quickly embrace. The decision to take on a plant-based meal plan is based on wanting to live healthier lives. The change might be inevitable later on after many realizations of what we get when we eventually abandon what we prefer to consume. The previous chapters have narrowed down to health issues with many studies leading to a better life in adopting the latter meal plan, which is plant-sourced.

Changing from regular life diets to start incorporating plant-based foods will meet some resistance at first if not well understood. It is now through this that we have come up with different tips to follow to start a plant-based diet. These several tips can help us and make our understanding much more comfortable when dealing with plant-based foods. These tips also are used as guidelines that will help us not only today but even in the coming generations.

With that said, some people prefer a diet full of meat just because of its taste than understanding the health issues associated with its high consumption. These tips have been explained below in detail. The following chapters keenly highlight the need for easier comprehension. So that each one of us can be in a better position to indulge in eating the plant-based plant meals, after all, all of us need to begin from somewhere.

The first tip is all about setting rules and making sure that you are being initiated to new recipes of plant-based meals even twice a week. Regulations created by yourself will be quickly followed as compared to the ones formed and forced on you. In this plant-based diet, it is all about loving what you are doing. The created recipes will always be easy to follow, and once mastered, you will only be improving on them. One rule that can be created here is the setting of a day. This day is preserved mainly for one purpose and that's making a plant-based meal. Make it to the family and get their ultimate reviews on what you have done. Ask them to comment on the tastes and the food in general. The result will help you a lot, especially in your next meal.

The next tip here is all about creating a constant tendency towards plant-based meals. Make a plan for cooking this food more often within a week. Don't wait for ages to pass since you re getting induced to starting your plant-based diet. Practice makes perfect, and within a long time, your skills, especially necessary skills, will improve. Your experience will be a notch higher, and this will be reflected in your habits. Making cooking of plant meals frequent is one of the most excellent tips in jump-starting your plant-based meal. Along the way, you will get adapted to it. You'll also realize that you've changed your approach to how you always think of other types of food, such as diets full of meat and junk foods.

It's vital to grab recipes from the shelves or drawers where they are kept and reading. The habit can occur without necessarily making or preparing these foods. At the same time, the pattern can improve your skills and give you several tips and morale to embark on preparation later on. Reading equips one with the required skills and creativity needed in an area of expertise. After having enough knowledge and comprehension, especially on these plant-based recipes, you can now embark on that kitchen work. Follow your recipes slowly by slowly and get used to it after some trials. The action will make it even easier. You will start enjoying it, and without knowing, you will be in an excellent position to begin migrating from your current diet to plant-based diets.

Most of us usually use vegetables in our daily diets without knowing their value. They may also use the plants in meal preparation without having a rare view of what they do in our food. Some use vegetables because others have been using while some will try to incorporate it just because it is there. It is just well for your understanding about this, but if you want to jump-start into this diet, then go for the vegetables that people regard as unusual.

The ones that you have never used ever since you were born. The ones you have never even seen. Visit different fruits vendors store and have these unusual collections. Ask questions if in case you do not understand. Pick them and try using them already to check on their flavors and tastes. Your ability to pick the right plant-based meal plan will help you to choose which to use and not to use. It is good to note that these unusual vegetables can be used to compensate for flavors gotten from meat-related dishes. This choosing of particular types of plants is a good tip to start your plant-based diet.

As a beginner in this diet, the best tip for starting a plant-based diet meal plan will be, to begin with, vegetables. Try as much as possible to eat vegetables. The act can be during lunch and dinner or rather a supper. Make sure that your plate is always full of plants of different categories. Don't wait for ages to pass since you are getting induced to starting your plant-based diet. Practice makes perfect, and within a long time, your skills, especially necessary skills, will improve. Your experience will be a notch higher, and this will be reflected in your habits. Making cooking of plant meals frequent is one of the most excellent tips in jump-starting your plant-based meal. Along the way, you will get adapted to it.

Different colors can help you choose the different types you want to get to learn. Vegetables too can also be eaten as snacks, especially when combined with hummus or salsa. You can also use guacamole too in this combination and rest assured you will love it.

People eat meat, and it has been part and parcel of their daily diet. As said earlier, many prefer meat due to its taste. They don't go for it because of its nutritional value. In many cases, we can ook for ways to change our thinking about meat. If we can all agree to reduce the level of intake of meat, our lives would be better. The reason is appended to the health benefits of taking vegetables and not meat.

Then, the same can be replaced with the high intake of the plant-based meal, and then we shall rest assured that at long last our thinking about meat will have to change. For us to improve our diet, then we need to know the side effects of taking meat in large quantities. One of the most dangerous side effects is its ability to build up within the body tissues. Together with fatty oils, your body loses shape and obesity will encroach. Don't wait for ages to pass since you are getting induced to starting your plant-based diet. Practice makes perfect, and within a long time, your skills, especially necessary skills, will improve. Your experience will be a notch higher, and this will be reflected in your habits. Making cooking of plant meals frequent is one of the most excellent tips in jump-starting your plant-based meal. Along the way, you will get adapted to it.

Life-threatening problems start arising, and this will only land you into the hospital as you seek medication. In the long run, your life will be affected by the economic challenges appended to it. As you realize you have wasted many resources in dealing with a condition, you could have controlled from the beginning. The action might cause some depression and stress. It's good to note that you are not supposed to withdraw all meat at once. In this case, you can change your approach towards meal intake. Reducing the level of consumption will help us to indulge in plant-based cooking meals plan. You can also use this meat as just a side dish. That's like garnish. Avoid using meat as a centerpiece.

The types of fats and oils being used should be highly considered. Well-Chosen fats or oils will come from avocados, olive oil, some specific seeds and even nuts like groundnuts and so on. By doing this, you will be in a high position of being initiated to plant-based cooking.

As we all know, changing from one diet to another diet will be challenging. The case is specific, especially within a short period. What you need to do is to cook at least twice, thrice or even once within a week. Cook some plant-based food once or twice a week depending on how you might want.

You will learn how to jump-start your initiation period. You'll also understand what it takes to grasp the basic knowledge of plant-based meal planning.

In most cases, try to use more vegetables, beans, and even whole grains. Never use processed foodstuffs like processed and refined flour since this has got fewer nutrients and mostly lacks enough fiber needed within the body.

Another tip that will help you in starting a plant-based diet meal is by using whole grains during breakfast. Use it in high quantities since it will help you in adopting this kind of diet within a short period. It is not always easy to use all of these whole grains. The best way forward is to choose meals that can suit you and the rest of your family at first. Good examples will be highly recommended. These might include oats, barley, or even buckwheat. Here, you can add some flavors provided by different types of nuts and several seeds. Don't forget to include fresh fruits next to your reach.

Greens are some of the best vegetables preferable in the plant-based diet. They are also crucial in helping you to maintain a healthy diet. And going for them will help you jump start your long journey in embracing plant-based foods. Greens can be used at different levels and embracing it at the initial level is the best. Go for greens such as kales, spinach, collards and much more.

Use a good mode of cooking to preserve their nutritional value and also their tastes and flavors. Excellent cooking methods of food can include the use of steam, grilling, or even frying for a short period. All the mentioned styles of cooking or somewhat preparation will help in maintaining the nutrients found in these greens. The body tissues readily require these nutrients for the proper functionality of the body organs.

Another way to get induced to a plant-based diet is by using diets that revolve or contains salad. You can make the salad greens from leafy greens like spinach, romaine and sometimes the red leafy greens are preferred. Different kinds of vegetables are added here. These vegetables are added together with beans, peas, or even fresh herbs.

The best thing with fruits is that fruits can be consumed at any time and in any way. They don't have any form of rigid procedure or protocol that needs to be followed as far as their consumption is concerned. Eating fruits every day as dessert will help you get adapted to it. Don't wait for ages to pass since you are getting induced to starting your plant-based diet. Practice makes perfect, and within a long time, your skills, especially necessary skills, will improve. Your experience will be a notch higher, and this will be reflected in your habits. Making cooking of plant meals frequent is one of the most excellent tips in jump-starting your plant-based meal. Along the way, you will get adapted to it.

This will create some sorts of habits within you and without realizing you will be fully indulged in a plant-based meal.

Fruits play different roles in our diet plans. By consuming them every day, we can quickly boost our immunity. The same meals will help us to forget to focus more on eating healthy for the rest of our lives. For example, some fruits will help you reduce the level of craving for sugary sweets, especially after having the main meal. Fruits such as watermelon and apples can help in keeping hydrated. Therefore, you will be able to get used to it. Within the long run, you will be adapted to plant-based diet meals.

Another way that can also help you start your meal plan is by having curiosity or instead of being extra curious. Many studies have solid proof of interest as a tip in starting plant-based meal plans. Sometimes in life, you want to venture into something you never knew. You want to do something that you have not been doing, especially when it comes to cooking different meal plans.

Many times people have been obsessed with junk food and other meat-related foods. Trying something new is just out of curiosity and may take a reasonable period to understand fully. In the long run, you will develop skills that will eventually help you to do every work within the kitchen. Don't wait for ages to pass since you are getting induced to starting your plant-based diet. Practic makes perfect, and within a long time, your skills, especially necessary skills, will improve. Your experience will be a notch higher, and this will be reflected in your habits. Making cooking of plant meals frequent is one of the most excellent tips in jump-starting your plant-based meal. Along the way, you will get adapted to it.

s has been said earlier, changing from your healthy diet to a
lant-based diet is not simple. However, after an extended
eriod, you will be in an excellent position to embrace it. This
omes about after your curiosity to do something new every day.
ou will get used to it over time.

ometimes you can jump-start this plant meal as a result of love.
Iany people are trying something new. If you have that love for
lant-related dishes, then you will be in an excellent position to
mbrace it after some time. The move will help you manage your
ating habits.

mbracing plant-based diet meal plans will come in handy with
ie broader choice of the food sector to choose from. You will
ave an alternative source of food in addition to what you have
een consuming over the last years. Having led by your love to
at plant-based meals or rather to change the diet will vastly help
ou to get used to it.

Vithin the long run, you will get familiarized and used to it. You
ill then start practicing it in your daily routines, thus reducing
our urge on meat-related meals. For this one to work better, you
1ust love eating too. The eventual result is just an aspect of life

that will accelerate your objective in starting plant-based diet meal plans.

Another tip is about pairing foods. You can use this tool to have more excellent knowledge of which types of plant-based foods can be matched and results in good taste. You can do this pairing by combining several flavors. The result should give you a strong feeling that works for you.

The same is appended to the fact that trial and error works. When you comprehend food pairing completely, rest assured that your cooking skills and love of it are moving to the next level. The later will even enable you to cook your plant-based meal without checking or following your recipes. You shall also experience timely results in time reduction and saves energy too. Sometimes you need also to compare notes on different books about plant-based recipes and pick only the best that can help you begin on this.

You can choose a paper having a Mediterranean diet and another one having vegetarian food recipes or you can also go for the Nordic diet. Compare the notes and pick the similarities. The actions will make you understand much more about plant-based food and how to adequately prepare them. These books done by different authors will also help you with some inspiration and ideas on different flavors.

Watching is also regarded as another tip, which will help you to start plant-based meal plans. Have those videos concerning cooking at your reach. Several stations are dealing with cooking. Spend much time watching them as you dearly take notes. Make a date with your television and watch those food networks that talk much about plant-based diets.

Many studies have concluded that cooking videos are essential tools, especially in cooking. This is because, in your mind, you will be in a position to know how the food will look like even if you are not cooking. Using videos create some perfection in the kitchen. You'll have no stress or pressure here. It is all about watching and doing the required practice. Practicing now and then gives you that experience you need and will later help you to get embraced to the plant-based diet.

Your body is transitioning in this diet as well. If you're not watching your intake, you may end up deficient in one or many things and this will harm your health. You can even go through what is called the keto flu. The keto flu is what happens when your body begins adjusting to running on a different ratio of macronutrients than it used to. You begin to experience flu-like symptoms and experience stomach pain, dizziness, brain fog, diarrhea, constipation, muscle cramps, trouble sleeping, sugar cravings, the inability to stay asleep, or lack of focus and concentration. This doesn't happen to everyone, but it is something to be aware of.

Vegans need calcium and vitamin D especially. Calcium is vital for maintaining strong bones and teeth. As you're still eating and consuming dairy foods on this diet, you will be able to get calcium into your system pretty easily. Greens are also a good source of calcium. Broccoli and kale are really good examples. Another is turnips and collard greens. Just remember what veggies are best for the ketogenic diet as well. In a ketogenic diet during the early stages when you're losing more calcium (because of the transitioning process where you're losing electrolytes), you will need more amounts of calcium as you're losing that too.

Vitamin D is also good for bone health. Since milk is high in both sugar and carbs and not good for ketogenic, you should try to find your vitamin D in cereal if you can. If you're still not getting enough vitamin D and you don't get out in the sun much, you will probably need a supplement to help you get the right amount. They offer plant derived ones as well which is essential in a vegan diet where you do not use anything derived from animals.

Vitamin B12 or cyanocobalamin is necessary to produce red blood cells. This vitamin is important because it forms the red blood cell in your body. It also helps with the fatty acids in your body by breaking them down to produce vital energy that you will be able to use throughout your day. It's the most well-known B vitamin for a reason. It is also helpful with mental clarity and used to prevent anemia. Anemia is a condition that happens when you have a red blood cell deficiency or a deficiency of hemoglobin in the blood. This results in weariness and pallor. Pallor means you have an unhealthy pale appearance. So vitamin D is going to be a big issue if you're not getting enough as anemia can cause an entire host of problems. On a vegan ketogenic diet, you don't get very much leeway here. Eggs and milk both contain B12. It is not generally found in plant foods, but you can find it in fortified breakfast cereals. The problem is you can't have dairy. This means you would be finding it in your fortified cereals but that would not be enough for a vegan. If you find that you are not getting the amount that you need with these foods, you will need to find a supplement to correct it.

Zinc is important because it has a part in the formations of the proteins in your body as well as playing a role in cell division. It also has a part to play as an elemental part of the enzymes that are inside you. Zinc is more easily absorbed from animal products, but it can be absorbed from plant sources as well, though just not quite as easily. For a plant source of zinc, you've got choices from whole grains, wheat germ, soy products, and nuts. Most nuts are high in carbs though, so you might not want to choose that option unless you're willing to possibly go too high in carbohydrates.

Nutrients and micronutrients are going to be really important for you in this lifestyle because missing out on them can make you really sick and cause deficiencies in your body that would need to be corrected right away. The deficiencies can cause some serious issues and in some cases, life-threatening issues.

Micronutrients are nutrients that are needed for the human body. You usually need these in trace amounts. These micronutrients are part of development and growth. This is normal for the human body. This includes minerals, fatty acids, antioxidants, trace elements, and vitamins. Micronutrients your body protect itself from getting sick or help fight off diseases. These also ensure that the parts of your body under its care are being protected and functioning the way they're supposed to. This is a definite plus since these are in charge of almost every system in your body. Macronutrients, on the other hand, is a substance that is required in relatively large amounts by living organisms. Another way of describing it would be a type of food like a protein, fat, or carbs that are required in large amounts in the human diet.

A perfect example is processed food. Take cookies for example. A popular brand contains virtually zero micronutrients. Instead, it's mainly composed of carbohydrates, meaning, it's something to steer clear of on a ketogenic diet. They can also drastically spike your blood sugar. On the other side of this spectrum, foods such as leafy greens that you can consume on this diet are a great way to get your micronutrients. These include vitamin A, omega threes, and potassium.

The reason that you're making sure of getting the essential vitamins is that on the ketogenic diet, it can be low in micros if you are only trying to hit certain goals and not all of them. One thing to remember is that you need both your micronutrients and macronutrients. You still need micronutrients and its value in your diet. Knowing how to compose meals that are rich in nutrients is important and will be a key factor in this diet and vegetables are really going to help you get it in as these are full of them.

Chapter 2: Benefits of a plant based diet

Weight loss

If you are trying to lose weight, it's time to bring some change with a plant-based diet. These nutrient-dense food items can help you lose weight effectively, as you consume a fewer calories naturally by following a plant-based diet.

So many weight-loss diets focus on avoiding, losing, reducing. This makes you feel deprived and shortchanged. Negativity and self-deprecation will raise your stress levels and affect your health and quality of life.

Despite the dedication to counting calories, tracking steps, going to the gym, and diets that eliminate everything we love or add a "miracle" supplement, our society is increasingly afflicted with obesity and the diseases that result from it. Deprivation dieting isn't a successful long-term strategy, and calorie restriction slows our metabolism, making it harder to maintain any weight loss.

A simpler and more effective way to approach weight loss is to think of foods in terms of nutrient density and calorie density. To lose weight, you increase your proportion of nutrient-dense food and decrease your proportion of junk foods. The magic of this approach is that it flips the focus to the positive of creating health for yourself by eating more of the delicious, satisfying good stuff.

Nutrient-dense foods have a high amount of vitamins, minerals, and antioxidants for their volume. Vegetables, fruit, whole grains, beans, herbs, and spices are all nutrient-dense foods. Calorie-dense foods have a high amount of calories for their volume. Some examples are oils, sugars, dairy, eggs, oily fish, meat, and fried foods.

There are some foods that are both nutrient and calorie dense, like nuts, seeds, and avocados. You want to eat those foods because they have important minerals and other nutrients, and small amounts can help you feel full. You just need to eat them in smaller portions than you do other nutrient-dense foods.

Some foods are lacking in nutrients, even though they add calories to your day. These are called empty-calorie foods. They leave your body still craving nutrients, even though you've added calories to your day. White rice, white bread, refined oils, and refined sugar are examples.

Going plant based and focusing on choosing whole foods over processed or refined versions boosts nutrient density while lowering calorie density. It will also increase your water and fiber intake, both of which boost your metabolism and improve your digestion.

All the elements of the diet work together to satisfy and nourish the body on a deep level, so you thrive while you naturally lose weight. Over time, you'll find that those intense cravings you used to have for junk foods just fall away, as you feel the energy and health you're building. You're adding and expanding, not denying and taking away, so you feel abundant, happy, and fulfilled.

Maintain your Weight

If not planned properly, the side effects of mineral deficiencies will not only affect physical growth but mental health as well. Vegetarian diets, as opposed to vegan diets, do consume higher quantities of calcium and vitamin B_{12} due to the fact that they would not necessarily remove dairy and eggs from their diets (the main sources of these micronutrients in aforementioned diets).

By actively focusing on nutrition, both vegans and vegetarians are able to increase the effectiveness with which their bodies are able to absorb nutrients from plant-based sources. Additionally, this strategy could be combined with the intake of supplements, especially for iron and vitamins D and B_{12} (Appleby et al., 2007). Having your blood nutrient levels measured by your general practitioner and subsequently keeping track of your daily intake, you will be able to safely and happily follow a completely plant-based diet with all the accompanying benefits.

Incorporating more plants into your diet will reduce the risk of health-related problems, such as diabetes and heart disease. It is also effective for controlling and maintaining weight.

The most important takeaway from this is that while a vegan diet is better in supporting weight loss, improving overall health, and reducing risks of many diseases, if not properly planned, there is a risk of severe nutrient deficiencies (Petre, 2016).

Controlled Blood Sugar Levels

Also being a diet low in fat, devoid of junk foods, artificial sugars and sweetened foods, the vegetarians have a lower possibility of suffering from abnormal blood sugar levels which often results in diabetes. A study released by the George Washington University School of Medicine confirmed that a vegetarian's diet plays a vital role in maintaining blood sugar levels which invariably, reduces the chances of suffering from diabetes.

Control Appetite

There are so many appetizing and tasty plant food options out there that you may not even know about! Many of us are so accustomed to meat, animal products and processed foods taking center-stage at meal times that it is hard to imagine what a meal that puts plant foods first would look like. Embarking on a plant-based diet provides you an exciting opportunity to explore new foods and recipes that are not only satisfying and nourishing but are delicious and taste amazing as well.

Improve Brain Function

People who consume plant-based products have a lower risk of developing diseases or having strokes because of the fiber, vitamins and minerals that come along with a plant-based diet. The fiber, vitamins and minerals, as well as healthy fats, are essential substances your body needs in order to function properly. Plant-based diet thus improve the blood lipid levels and better your brain health as well. There is a significant decrease in bad cholesterol in people who follow a plant-based diet.

Improves Sleeps

Your body is transitioning in this diet as well. If you're not watching your intake, you may end up deficient in one or many things and this will harm your health. You can even go through what is called the keto flu. The keto flu is what happens when your body begins adjusting to running on a different ratio of macronutrients than it used to. You begin to experience flu-like symptoms and experience stomach pain, dizziness, brain fog, diarrhea, constipation, muscle cramps, trouble sleeping, sugar cravings, the inability to stay asleep, or lack of focus and concentration. This doesn't happen to everyone, but it is something to be aware of.

Improve Digestion

With a massive boost in fiber, most people find their digestion improves. Many of my clients find that their pants fit better simply from a less bloated stomach.

Cholesterol

Plants don't contain cholesterol, which includes saturated forms such as coffee or chocolate. When you live a plant-based diet lifestyle, you're reducing the amount of cholesterol you take in to next to zero.

HeaLth Disease

Following a plant-based diet is likely to reduce the risk of cardiovascular diseases, and enhance other risk factors for heart disease by reducing cholesterol, and blood pressure, and enhancing the blood sugar control. Following a plant-based diet can also help quell inflammation, which increases the risk of heart diseases by regulating plaque buildup in the arteries.

Longevity

While science cannot fully prove that particular diets result in increased life span, the benefits of such diets like the plant-based one to general health offers such opportunities.

Imagine a body free of different ailments, it stands a chance of living longer than one battered with diseases.

For example, hypertension happens to be common killer of lives across the globe. Since, the plant-based diet targets reducing and avoiding hypertension, this problem is highly curbed on a large scale.

Many other treatments of diseases like diabetes, cancers, etc. are excellent contribution to cases of increased longevity by the plant-based diet.

Chapter 3: Guidelines and rules for eating Plant Based Diet

Mistakes to avoid

Settling in with a new diet plan is always a confusing experience, but with time and understanding, anyone can avoid repeating the same mistakes over and over again. The following are a few common mistakes people make on the plant-based diet:

More Focus on Carbohydrates:

Plants do not only contain carbohydrates; there is a range of nutrients that can be consumed by ingesting a variety of plant-based food. People end up consuming more carbohydrates, and it simply adds to their obesity, which is not healthy. Limit yourself to carbohydrate intake as per your actual needs.

Compromising on Proteins

People falsely believe that proteins can only be sourced from animal products, and that plants cannot provide proteins—which is far from the truth! Plant-based food, like most beans and lentils, contain a high amount of proteins, do don't compromise on protein intake.

Processed Meal

Remember, the plant-based diet does not mean you should avoid only animal-based food, but it mainly prevents you from eating anything not sourced from plants, and that includes processed meals. Avoiding such items is necessary in order to harness the true benefits of the diet.

Refined Carbs

Like saturated fats, refined carbs are also not healthy, as they simply raise blood sugar levels and are obtained by processing complex carbs. Their intake should be limited to the plant-based diet.

Omega 3

Fish and seafood are not the only sources of omega 3; people on plant-based diet often forget this fact and do not care to find better Omega 3 substitutes. Seeds and nuts are also a good source of omega 3, and they can be eaten frequently on this diet to meet needs.

Supplements

The US recommended daily allowance (RDA) for vitamin B_{12} is 2.4 micrograms per day for most adults and 2.8 micrograms for pregnant or nursing women. More recent studies put the ideal intake higher, at 4 to 7 micrograms per day. I suggest looking for maple sugar, date sugar, or even cane sugar. On top of these options, you can always choose pure maple syrup. The goal is to make sure that you're getting real maple syrup and not something that is maple-flavored.

Since B vitamins stimulate energy and the nervous system, it's better to take them in the morning and early afternoon so that you don't get wired before going to sleep.

Researchers are also starting to link vitamin D deficiency with all kinds of health problems and diseases, including asthma and cancer. Meat-eaters should be just as concerned here. The results of a 2009 study showed that the majority of both vegetarians (59 percent) and meat-eaters (64 percent) do not have sufficient blood levels of vitamin D.

There's no vitamin D in plant foods, but our bodies produce it naturally when our skin is exposed to the sun. It's a hard thing to measure and rely on, though, since we produce different amounts depending on skin color and other factors. In the winter, we usually don't get as much sun exposure as we do in the summer. The farther north you are, the more winter will affect your vitamin D levels, and if you're really far north you may not get any in the winter. The baseline RDA is 600 IU a day, but for optimal health, supplementation in the range of 1,000 to 2,000 IU daily has been shown to be a good level for most people. Up to 4,000 IU is safe for most adults.

Meat Alternatives

For a rich, heart texture that will help to fill you up there is beans, Portobello mushrooms, tempeh, and tofu. Each of these are chewy and hearty, and they can be marinated to get different flavors. You can also use these for chili, stews, and burgers or can be served baked.

Replace fish with flaxseed. Seafood contains heavy metals like mercury, as well as microplastics from our polluted oceans. About 90 million to 100 million tons of fish are taken from the ocean every year, and for each pound of fish there is up to 5 pounds of bycatch. (That's fish that are caught up unintentionally in nets.) We could see fishless oceans by 2048.

Egg Alternatives

Turmeric

Turmeric gives a light yellow color when used in preparing egg-free dishes. It comes as a small root or in powdered form, and it is known to have anti-inflammatory properties. Turmeric can easily be purchased at grocery stores, and a little will provide an egg-like color to your food.

Apple Sauce

Making use of apple sauce is another way to substitute eggs in baked foods without adding eggs. Make use of a 1/4 cup of apple sauce (unsweetened) to replace a single egg. Apple sauce adds flavor and moisture to foods like cakes, bread, cookies, and muffins. However, they can be bought in stores or self-made by making use of fresh apples.

Black Salt (Kala namak)

Black salt is a volcanic salt that is used in Asian culinary art. As a result of it's concentrated sulfur content, it has a powerful flavor that tastes like eggs, making it a common ingredient used by vegans. It works brilliantly in vegan egg salads, tofu scrambles, vegan french toast, quiches, and frittatas. Black salt can be purchased online or at specialty stores.

Egg Substitute Powders

Various alternatives for egg substitute powders can be purchased in multiple stores. Vegan, gluten-free, and versatile, they usually contain flour or starch and a raising agent. They are also an excellent substitute for eggs when the volume is important. These powders won't add unwanted sweetness or flavor, and they can be used in cakes, muffins, cookies, and also as a building agent in vegan meatloaves or casseroles.

Tapioca Starch

Tapioca starch is used as a thickening or binding agent for condiments, sauces, and puddings. Make use of 1 tbsp of tapioca stare, grounded with 3 tbsp of water to substitute one egg. Tapioca starch is used to manufacture vegan mayonnaise, which is creamy and smooth, and it is considered to be a baking ingredient for most people.

Cheese Alternatives

For Mozzarella — make use of daiya cheese:

The mouthwatering texture and stringiness of mozzarella can be difficult to prepare at home. However, this is why a dairy-free cheese such as 'Daiya' is recommended. I suggest looking for maple sugar, date sugar, or even cane sugar. On top of these options, you can always choose pure maple syrup. The goal is to make sure that you're getting real maple syrup and not something that is maple-flavored.

Made with arrowroot, tapioca starch, potato protein isolate, and coconut oil, Daiya's shredded mozzarella (dairy-free) is the best option for making tacos, salads, pizzas, and quesadillas. Tapioca, which is gotten from root vegetable cassavas, can be used to represent a thickening agent in lots of food products, which include vegan cheese. It is easier to prepare and has the same healthy texture, but it stretches and melts.

For Blue Cheese — make use of herb and garlic cashew cheese:

If you prefer the spiciness of stilton or you prefer the nutty and sharp flavors of Gorgonzola, there are various kinds of blue cheese you can add to your dishes. The use of nutritional yeast, fresh minced dill, and garlic powder gives cashew cheese a tasty look and a great taste, which is comparable to Roquefort blue cheese. Dish with whole-grain crackers and crudites for a delicious wine along with faux-cheese spread.

For Ricotta Cheese — make use of almond cheese:

Almonds are known to be the perfect substitute for creamy cheeses like goat cheese, ricotta, and cream cheese. They have a subtle nut flavor that goes along with a variety of herbs and spices. To prepare almond cheese, soak 1 cup of almonds in clean water for a minimum of one hour. Then blend along with 1/3 cup of water, grounded black pepper, salt, and lemon juice. You can tune the flavor by including ingredients, such as minced garlic, dijon mustard, and natural yeast.

Milk Alternatives

Lots of plant-based milk alternatives are as nutrients as typical dairy milk when consumed moderately. It is essential to stop the consumption of cow milk because it can negatively affect your health. The list below shows the best alternatives for dairy milk:

Coconut Milk

This is a great duty-free alternative that can be easily gotten in grocery stores. It is manufactured by grinding coconut meat, and is also a great source of nutrients like potassium, magnesium, and iron. Coconut milk also contains a medium-chain fatty acid called lauric acid, which is used by the body for energy. It is essential to know that full-fat coconut milk contains excess calories, yet it provides lots of health benefits; therefore you should consume little portions.

Goat Milk

Although goat milk is considered to be dairy but it is still an excellent alternative for those looking to stay away from cow products. Goat milk can be a bit different to digest, make you feel bloated, or affect your skin, yet it causes less digestive issues and inflammation than cow milk. Goat milk is endowed with adequate unsaturated fatty acids and also contain more medium-chain and short-chain fatty acids.

Almond Milk

This is a blend of water and finely ground almonds, which are a great alternative to dairy milk. It doesn't contain lactose, gluten or soy proteins, and it has anti-inflammatory properties. Unlike dairy milk, almond milk is more comfortable to digest, but almond milk is that it is often fortified with many additional nutrients and sweetened with added sugar. However, you should always go for organic, plain almond milk or you can decide to make it yourself.

How to eat out

It can be hard to dine out when you're trying to enjoy a plant-based diet. However, there are many restaurants that offer vegan options, so try to look for one in advance. Just realize that you'll need to minimize the number of times you eat out. However, if you need to go out then check out the menu online before you arrive. Look for dishes that are low in fat and full of vegetables, and then look for grilled, baked and steamed options. Try to avoid any dishes that are fried, rich, creamy or crispy. Just don't be shy about asking for a different salad dressing or side dish either. Make sure sauces and cheeses are left out too. If there's bread, ask for whole wheat. If there is rice, ask for brown rice.

Macro and micronutrients intake

Foods are made up of a mix of macronutrients (carbohydrates, fats, and proteins) and micronutrients (vitamins and minerals). The largest component of your daily intake should be carbohydrates. Fat makes up the next largest section, followed closely by protein. Since fats give you twice as much energy for the same volume, when looking at the portion size, fat and protein should be about equal.

Most people should aim for 60 to 70 percent carbohydrates, 20 to 30 percent fat, and 10 to 15 percent protein in their daily diet, with up to 20 percent protein for elite athletes. If your energy needs are about 1,500 calories, which I find to be the average of my clients, that works out to 225 to 263 grams of carbohydrates, 33 to 50 grams of fat, and 38 to 56 grams of protein per day. The specific percentage that works for you may be at the higher or lower end of those ranges, but the ranges are appropriate for about 98 percent of the population. Where you fall within the ranges may change a bit throughout your life and throughout the seasons of the year, so listen to your body. Despite some popular diet guides, there's most likely no benefit in going outside of these ranges. Even the biggest bodybuilders never need more than 20 percent protein, and it can in fact be harmful to your kidneys and general metabolism.

If you're like most people, though, you don't look at foods as carbohydrates or fats—but as rice or avocados. The cool thing about plant foods is that they're much more nutritionally balanced than animal foods, so it's easier to stay within the normal ranges listed earlier without having to meticulously track what you're eating. Let's look at the proportions of macronutrients in whole plant foods.

Carbohydrates

Some people worry about consuming too many carbohydrates by eating plant foods. Carbohydrates are your body's main source of energy and are completely healthy if you eat them in the form of whole foods (such as whole grains, vegetables, and fruit), since they contain lots of vitamins, minerals, antioxidants, water, and fiber. Fiber is also a carbohydrate, but its role is to facilitate digestion rather than give energy.

Whole grains and fruit have the highest levels of carbohydrates, with about 70 to 90 percent carbohydrate content. Eating a banana is an instant energy boost. The best food sources of fiber are psyllium or flaxseed and leafy green vegetables.

Protein

It's not nearly as hard as people think to get enough protein from plant foods. All whole plant foods have some protein in them. If you eat enough calories from a balanced and varied diet, and include legumes regularly, you should get more than enough protein and all the essential amino acids (which are the building blocks of protein). You do not have to combine different foods in a single meal to get the essential amino acids all together—a common misconception. If you eat different foods within 48 hours, the amino acids will get together to do their job.

Legumes, including beans, have the highest overall protein content of plant foods at about 18 to 25 percent; they are also important in plant-based diets because they provide enough of the amino acid lysine. Dark green leafy vegetables have a high proportion of protein at 40 percent, spices add tiny but important amounts of amino acids, and whole grains add a fair amount of protein to an overall balanced diet at 8 to 12 percent.

Fats

Your body needs enough dietary fat to function, maintain metabolism, and absorb and utilize minerals and certain vitamins. People with cold hands and feet, amenorrhea (missed menstrual periods), or dry skin, hair, or throat may need more fats in their diet, and particularly saturated fats like coconut oil. To be clear, eating healthy fat in reasonable amounts doesn't make you fat.

The best source of healthy fat is whole plant foods—avocados, nuts, and seeds (including nut and seed butters). These average about 80 percent fat. Whole grains and beans also have some healthy fat, and there are even small amounts in fruits, vegetables, spices, and pretty much every food. Oats, for example, are about 15 percent fat.

Oils are 100 percent fat and aren't something you necessarily need to eat, but they are great for carrying rich flavor and mouthfeel in a dish, particularly when you're transitioning to a healthier diet. If you use oils, it's best to keep them minimal and use unrefined oils like olive, coconut, sesame, and avocado. Refined oils include canola, soy, sunflower, and corn oil.) You can easily sauté vegetables for two people with just a teaspoon of oil.

That doesn't mean you should never eat oils, though, and some people can actually benefit from concentrated fats. For example, flax oil or concentrated DHA might be necessary for someone with issues digesting and utilizing omega-3 fatty acids.

Fresh fruit and vegetable nutrient rich

Fruits

Like vegetables, fruit also has high water and fiber content and lots of vitamins and minerals. Fruit is an important source of quick energy, as it is digested and used by your body the fastest o any food group. Fruits contain concentrated antioxidants, and because they're sweet they're often more enjoyable than vegetables—particularly for kids.

Tree fruit is available in the summer and fall and includes apples, pears, plums, and peaches. Citrus fruit is best in the winter and includes oranges, grapefruit, lemons, and limes. Pure juice from citrus fruits can be used to flavor many plant-based recipes, including those using vegetables. Summer fruits include berries, grapes, and melon. Tropical fruits include bananas, pineapple, mango, and kiwi.

Vegetables

Nothing is better than a meal prepared with fresh vegetables. Vegetables are the key to a healthy life in a vegetarian lifestyle because, they are a great source of fiber, iron, sodium, potassium minerals, and vitamins that greatly help in controlling body weight and lowering risks of cardiac diseases.

Portion: Have 4 servings of vegetables per day, about 1 cup of rav veggies or 1/2 cup cooked. Ensure to have one calcium-rich greer vegetable on your plate like spinach or kale.

Plant Based Diet what eat

Now, we get to the fun part! If you still believe that a plant-base diet is going to be restrictive, be prepared to have your min changed forever. The truth is, the plant-based diet includes a wid variety of foods that you get to enjoy. I know so many people wh njoy this diet and the benefits that go along with it; isn't it about time you join them?

'o start off, we'll go over all of the incredible foods that you'll be njoying. After that, we'll go in depth on the foods you should void on the plant-based diet. As mentioned earlier, there's a nisconception that plant-based means no meat. That's wrong. 'ou can still have the meat. However, after reading about the roubles it can cause to your health and our dear planet, you night want to limit it or even give it a miss. Once you have verything you need to know, be sure to read the next chapter vhere I've created an expandable grocery list for you, some elicious recipes and even a simple meal plan to help you get tarted. I want to give you as much help as possible so success is loser than you think in your plant-based journey.

'oods to Eat Freely

ne of the major benefits of the plant-based diet is that you can ay goodbye to calorie counting! I mentioned earlier that the ods you'll be eating will be much more calorie-dense, meaning hat you'll feel fuller more easily and for a longer time! You can ay goodbye to counting calories and hello to actually enjoying our food! To begin, we will go over the foods that you can onsume freely.

ruits

Vhile all fruits are allowed, it should be noted that not all fruits re created equal. Each fruit provides its own unique health enefits and coming right up, you will get my compilation of me of the healthiest fruits for your plant-based diet.

Cranberries
Cranberries are unique fruits that are rich in vitamin K1, vitamin E, manganese, vitamin C, and copper! They also have a significant number of antioxidants that improve health significantly. Cranberries also contain A-type proanthocyanidins which **research** has shown, to be a great help in preventing gum inflammation and urinary tract infections.

Strawberries
Strawberries are among the most recommended fruits. On top of being delicious, it is also full of potassium, folate, manganese, and vitamin C. When compared to other fruits, strawberries are considered to have a low glycemic index, meaning they won't cause blood sugar spikes. **A study** published in the Anticancer Research journal has found that strawberries can actually prevent tumor growth.

Mango
Mango is an excellent fruit to add to your fruit list, especially in the summertime! Mango has soluble fiber and provides vitamin C, which makes it anti-inflammatory. It also has strong antioxidants that lower the risk of diseases. In animal **studies**, i was found that the compounds in mangos could help protect against diabetes.

Pomegranate
If you haven't had pomegranates before, you're missing out! Pomegranates are nutrient dense and have an excellent level of antioxidants to keep you healthy. In fact, a study published in the Journal of Agricultural and Food Chemistry has **found** that pomegranate juice has 3 times higher levels of antioxidants compared to red wine and green tea! On top of this, it's also full

of different kinds of polyphenols, which reduces the chance of developing cancer.

Apples

We have all heard it, an apple a day keeps the doctor away. As it turns out, there seems to be some truth to the saying! Apples are very nutritious and contain high amounts of vitamin K, potassium, vitamin C, and fiber! They also provide B vitamins. **Research** has shown that antioxidants found in apples can help promote heart health and may reduce the risk of Alzheimer's, cancer, and type 2 diabetes.

Blueberries

Blueberries are most commonly known for their high levels of antioxidants, but they are also high in manganese, vitamin K, vitamin C and fiber! Jam-packed with all these nutrients, it's no wonder blueberries can help **reduce** the risk of certain chronic conditions including diabetes and heart disease.

Pineapple

With just one cup of this delicious fruit, you receive all of the vitamin C you need for the day, plus a hefty amount of manganese too. Pineapple also has bromelain, which helps to digest proteins. In addition, **studies** have proven that pineapples can help fight and protect against cancer and tumor growth.

Grapefruit

The list of fruits you can enjoy goes on and on, but I'll end off with grapefruit. Grapefruit is one of the healthiest citrus fruits out there and is an excellent source of the vitamins and minerals. Research shows that grapefruit is **associated** with reduced cholesterol levels and may help prevent the forming of kidney stones.

Vegetables

On a plant-based diet, the bulk of what you'll be eating will be vegetables. Obviously, this does not come as a surprise. There are plenty of vegetables for you to enjoy, but the following are the real powerhouses that you'll want to include as often as possible into your diet.

Brussels Sprouts

Brussels sprouts are one of those vegetables that you absolutely love or loathe. The truth is, it is all in the preparation! Brussels sprouts contain an antioxidant known as kaempferol. This specific antioxidant is **linked** to the prevention of any cell damage that is caused by oxidative stress, and is an important antioxidant to keep chronic diseases at bay. Additionally, brussels sprouts are an excellent source of potassium, manganese, folate, and vitamin C, A and K!

Garlic

Rejoice all my garlic lovers! Garlic has many roots in our history as a medicinal plant. One of its main active compounds is allicin, and the research has shown that this **compound** helps to regulate blood sugar and promotes excellent heart health. It was also **found** in a study published in The American Journal of Clinical Nutrition that garlic is beneficial in lowering total blood cholesterol, LDL cholesterol, and triglycerides, all while increasing healthy HDL cholesterol.

Broccoli

Broccoli is a part of the cruciferous family. This vegetable is rich in vitamin C and vitamin K. It also contains an abundant amount of potassium, manganese, and folate, which we need daily. Broccoli also contains sulforaphane, which has been found to have a protective effect against cancer. In one **specific study**, sulforaphane was successfully able to reduce the number and size of breast cancer cells while simultaneously blocking tumor growth.

Carrots

In one cup of carrots, you'll receive 428% of your daily recommended vitamin A. Carrots also contain the antioxidant beta-carotene which is associated with cancer prevention. In fact, one **study** found that by eating one serving of carrots during a week could lower the risk of prostate cancer by 5%.

Spinach

Of course, spinach is on the list! Spinach tops the charts as being one of the healthiest vegetables, and it isn't hard to understand why! Spinach is rich in iron, vitamin A, vitamin K, and is also packed with antioxidants. It also contains the compound called carotenoid, which the research has shown, can help individuals reduce their risk of **cancer.**

Legumes

While beans and legumes are more known for their fiber and B vitamins, they're also the main source of protein for your new, plant-based diet. Now, I will list some of the healthier ones you should make into staples, or when you're looking to switch out those animal proteins.

Black Beans

Black beans might just become one of your new favorite foods. Not only are they packed with fiber and folate, they also offer 15.2 grams of protein in just one cup! These beans are beneficial as they have a lower glycemic index when compared to other foods with higher carbohydrates content. This means they can help control your blood sugar levels while being eaten as a staple. Scientists have even found evidence that black beans can **help** individuals manage their weight and type 2 diabetes.

Kidney Beans

These beans are another food that is fairly common on a plant-based diet. Comparable to black beans, a cup of kidney beans contains an impressive 13.4 grams of protein. They are also high in fiber and are known to help slow down the absorption of sugar into the bloodstream. In the same **study** mentioned earlier, it was found that there is a connection between kidney beans and type 2 diabetes as well. On top of that, the fiber in kidney beans also helped to reduce the spike in blood sugar after finishing a meal.

Peas

Peas are an excellent source of protein and fiber. They also have the ability to reduce insulin and blood sugar after a meal. What's more, you're not restricted to just plain peas anymore. Now, there is something called pea starch and it's also good for you. In fact, there is a **study** from the European Journal of Nutrition that discovered that pea starch could help you feel fuller for a longer amount of time.

Lentils

The next time someone asks how you get your protein on a plant-based diet, you'll know the answer is lentils. In one cup of lentils, you'll get a whopping 17.9 grams of protein! The research has shown that eating lentils helps to reduce blood sugar and lower the risk of **diabetes**. Another **study** published in The American Journal of Clinical Nutrition has even shown that lentils can improve gut health by increasing your bowel function. When the stomach is emptied at a quicker rate, digestion increases and spikes in blood sugar is prevented.

Chickpeas

The final source of protein that makes my list is chickpeas. They are often referred to as garbanzo beans and make an excellent source of fiber and protein. In one cup of chickpeas, you'll get 14.5 grams of protein. Specifically, chickpeas are great for reducing blood sugar levels and increasing sensitivity to insulin. It should also be noted that chickpeas can **help improve** bowel movement, by reducing the level of bad bacteria stuck in your intestines.

Whole Grains

As you switch to a plant-based diet, grains are going to become another staple in your household. Firstly, there are 3 types of whole grains – the bran, the germ, and the endosperm. Each one of these has its own nutrients, which are vital for your health. Whole grains are excellent as they are high in dietary fiber, B vitamins, selenium, phosphorus, manganese, magnesium, and iron! Here, I will share with you some of my favorites!

Quinoa

In South America, quinoa is a superfood! This is because this grain is packed with fiber, healthy fats, proteins and all the minerals and vitamins you need for a well-rounded diet. A **study** has shown that quinoa also contains the antioxidant kaempferol, (just like Brussels sprouts) and it helps in the prevention of certain types of cancers, heart disease and chronic inflammation

Brown Rice

For a majority of you, up until this point in your life, you've mostly been eating white rice. Yet, brown rice is the healthier alternative. This is because brown rice is a whole grain – it still has the bran and germ intact, which makes it richer in fiber, antioxidants, minerals, and vitamins. Along with these benefits, brown rice also happens to be gluten-free, which makes it an excellent choice if you need to follow a gluten-free diet.

Whole-grain Bread

On top of switching from white rice to brown rice, you'll also want to consider switching from white bread to whole-grain bread. There's a wide variety including whole-grain tortillas, bagels, rolls, and rye bread. Although it's a simple switch, you're actually adding more whole grains into your diet and this is extremely nutritious.

Foods to Limit

In this next section, I will list off the foods you should still eat, but in sparing amounts. This means that even though they're allowed and do provide great health benefits, it doesn't mean you should eat them every day. That's because they also add a high amount of fat into your diet. This is especially crucial if you're looking to lose weight.

Avocado

said the same thing you're probably saying to yourself right now: Avocado is a fruit? Indeed, it is, but they are very different from your typical fruit. While most fruits are high in carbohydrate, avocado is low in carbs and acts more as an excellent source of healthy fats. The nutrients found in avocado include monounsaturated fat and oleic acid, both of which research has shown to be **associated** with better heart health and reduced inflammation.

Nuts & Nut Butters

Nuts are also an excellent source of fiber and protein. They are also commonly used as a healthy snack option. However, they do contain a relatively high fat content. The fat found in nuts include monounsaturated fat, omega-6, and omega-3 polyunsaturated fat. It should be noted that these fats are considered healthy, but you'll still want to consume them in moderation.

Examples: Peanut Butter, Tahini. Cashew Butter, Almond Butter, Walnuts, Pistachios, Pecans, Peanuts, Coconut, Cashews, Almonds.

Seeds & Seed Butters

Just like nuts; seeds are a great snacking alternative. Seeds are extremely nutritious and are an excellent source of fiber. They could potentially help to lower your blood pressure, cholesterol levels, and blood sugar. However, it's true that there can be too much of a good thing. So, although seeds contain polyunsaturated fats and healthy monounsaturated fats, which are essentially good fats, they should still be limited. Examples: Sunflower Seeds, Sesame Seeds, Flaxseeds, Chia Seeds.

Beverages

It should be noted that water is going to be the best beverage for you, but it is completely understandable if you don't want to just drink water for the rest of your life. This is why the following beverages are allowed, but should be limited to only a few times per week

Fruit Juices

Unsweetened Plant Milk, eg. Soy Milk or Almond Milk

Processed Smoothies

Soy Yogurt

Dried Fruits

Dried fruits are more processed compared to their whole or raw versions. If you do include dried fruits in your diet, you'll want to make sure that they are unsulfured. Some examples of dried fruits you could try include: Raisins, Medjool Dates, Currants, Cherries, Blueberries, Apricots, or Apples.

Sweeteners

Adding a little sweetener is the secret ingredient to making yummy desserts or to satisfy your sweet tooth. However, you'll want to choose those that are minimally processed. I suggest looking for maple sugar, date sugar, or even cane sugar. On top of these options, you can always choose pure maple syrup. The goal is to make sure that you're getting real maple syrup and not something that is maple-flavored. These are very important differences you'll want to be conscious of when you start a plant-based diet.

Condiments

When it comes to condiments, you'll need to be selective as well. While there are plenty of options on the market, you'll still want to select condiments that are going to be compliant with your new diet. Some of my favorites include Hot Sauce, Wasabi Paste, Vegan Worcestershire Sauce, Apple Cider Vinegar and Tomato Sauce. In the next chapter, you'll be gifted with a thorough grocery list to help you get started on your new diet!

Chapter 4: Shopping List

Fruits and Vegetables

Fruits

Any whole fruits are available on the plant-based diet. However, it is recommended that you avoid dried fruits and juiced fruits because of the sheer amount of sugar it'll pack into your diet.

Vegetables: Non-Starchy

These vegetables are excellent for your body because they are packed with nutrients and will help to get you the vitamins you need. This includes your leafy greens such as kale, spinach, butter lettuce, etc. You can also use eggplant, zucchini, tomatoes, and brocco li as your non-starchy basics.

Vegetables: Starchy

This includes all types of potatoes, whole corn, legumes of all kinds. This consists of all beans and lentils, root vegetables, and

ven quinoa. These are filling parts of your meals, which are
acked with fiber.

xtras

'ou'll find that you need more than just fruits and vegetables for
our plant-based diet. Remember to stock up on the following.

olled Oats

laxseed

hia Seeds (These can be found online for cheaper than most
rocery stores)

uinoa

entils

eans (Uncooked is cheaper than canned)

weet Potatoes

oconut Flour

lmond Flour

lilk Alternatives (Almond, Soy or Coconut milk are cheapest.

ofu

ils (Olive Oil or Coconut Oil is both cheap, healthy options)

Ierbs and Spices

s far as spices are concerned, any spices are allowed. This
icludes dried spices and fresh herbs.

Spices and herbs are not only a way to add rich flavor to your dishes but they also have small amounts of important nutrients. A study of vegetarian males eating an Indian diet showed that they got between 3.9 and 7.9 percent of their essential amino acid requirements, along with about 6 percent of calcium and 4 percent of iron, just from the seasonings in their food.

Many spices have protein, and although it doesn't amount to much in terms of grams, it provides a source of some of the amino acids that may be low in plant foods. Popular spices that will add a world of flavor to your food include cumin, coriander, cinnamon, paprika, and nutmeg.

Herbs like parsley, cilantro, mint, ginger, and basil pack loads of nutrients, and are most beneficial and flavorful when you eat them fresh. Parsley gives women 22 percent of their daily vitamin C recommendation, and men 27 percent, in just 4 tablespoons. All fresh herbs, like leafy greens, have a high antioxidant and chlorophyll content, providing energy and helping your body neutralize free radicals.

How to shop on a budget

These are plant-based foods, but they aren't as healthy for you as other plants. So, while you can have them, it's recommended that you use these sparingly. This includes added sweeteners. Examples of added sweeteners are fruit juice concentrate, natural sugars, honey, and maple syrup. Pumpkin seeds, sesame seeds, sunflower seeds, and dried fruits should also be consumed on a limited basis. Coconuts and avocados as well. You should also limit your refined wheat protein or soy protein

Chapter 5: 28 Day Meal Plan

Day 1

Breakfast-<u>Chai Flavoured Quinoa</u>

Lunch- <u>Three Bean Pasta</u>

Dinner- <u>Black Bean Wrap with Hummus</u>

Day 2

Breakfast- <u>Spinach Tofu Scramble</u>

Lunch- <u>Tofu Bean Salad</u>

Dinner- <u>Cauliflower Bowl</u>

Day 3

Breakfast- <u>Chai Flavoured Quinoa</u>

Lunch- <u>Peanut Tofu Sauce Noodles</u>

Dinner- <u>Quinoa Edamame Salad</u>

Day 4

Breakfast- Cauliflower Porridge

Lunch- Bolognese Pasta

Dinner- Apple Lentil Salad

Day 5

Breakfast- Overnight Hemp Cereal

Lunch- Spaghetti with Chickpeas Meatballs

Dinner- Vegan Sloppy Joe

Day 6

Breakfast- Overnight Chia Oatmeal

Lunch- Peanut Tofu Sauce Noodles

Dinner- Quinoa Edamame Salad

Day 7

Breakfast- Quinoa Oatmeal

Lunch- Bolognese Pasta

Dinner- Apple Lentil Salad

Day 8

Breakfast-Chai Flavoured Quinoa

Lunch- Three Bean Pasta

Dinner- Black Bean Wrap with Hummus

Day 9

Breakfast- Spinach Tofu Scramble

Lunch- Tofu Bean Salad

Dinner- Cauliflower Bowl

Day 10

Breakfast- Chai Flavoured Quinoa

Lunch- Peanut Tofu Sauce Noodles

Dinner- Quinoa Edamame Salad

Day 11

Breakfast- Cauliflower Porridge

Lunch- Bolognese Pasta

Dinner- Apple Lentil Salad

Day 12

Breakfast- Overnight Hemp Cereal

Lunch- Spaghetti with Chickpeas Meatballs

Dinner- Vegan Sloppy Joe

Day 13

Breakfast- Overnight Chia Oatmeal

Lunch- Peanut Tofu Sauce Noodles

Dinner- Quinoa Edamame Salad

Day 14

Breakfast- Quinoa Oatmeal

Lunch- Bolognese Pasta

Dinner- Apple Lentil Salad

Day 15

Breakfast-Chai Flavoured Quinoa

Lunch- Three Bean Pasta

Dinner- Black Bean Wrap with Hummus

Day 16

Breakfast- Spinach Tofu Scramble

Lunch- Tofu Bean Salad

Dinner- Cauliflower Bowl

Day 17

Breakfast- Chai Flavoured Quinoa

Lunch- Peanut Tofu Sauce Noodles

Dinner- Quinoa Edamame Salad

Day 18

Breakfast- Cauliflower Porridge

Lunch- Bolognese Pasta

Dinner- Apple Lentil Salad

Day 19

Breakfast- Overnight Hemp Cereal

Lunch- Spaghetti with Chickpeas Meatballs

Dinner- Vegan Sloppy Joe

Day 20

Breakfast- Overnight Chia Oatmeal

Lunch- Peanut Tofu Sauce Noodles

Dinner- Quinoa Edamame Salad

Day 21

Breakfast- Quinoa Oatmeal

Lunch- Bolognese Pasta

Dinner- Apple Lentil Salad

Day 22

Breakfast-Chai Flavoured Quinoa

Lunch- Three Bean Pasta

Dinner- Black Bean Wrap with Hummus

Day 23

Breakfast- Spinach Tofu Scramble

Lunch- Tofu Bean Salad

Dinner- Cauliflower Bowl

Day 24

Breakfast- Chai Flavoured Quinoa

Lunch- Peanut Tofu Sauce Noodles

Dinner- Quinoa Edamame Salad

Day 25

Breakfast- Cauliflower Porridge

Lunch- Bolognese Pasta

Dinner- Apple Lentil Salad

Day 26

Breakfast- Overnight Hemp Cereal

Lunch- Spaghetti with Chickpeas Meatballs

Dinner- Vegan Sloppy Joe

Day 27

Breakfast- Overnight Chia Oatmeal

Lunch- Peanut Tofu Sauce Noodles

Dinner- Quinoa Edamame Salad

Day 28

Breakfast- Quinoa Oatmeal

Lunch- Bolognese Pasta

Dinner- Apple Lentil Salad

Week 1 shopping list

Sage Leaves

Cloves Garlic

Onion

Olive Oil

Red Potatoes

Black Beans

Parsley

Swiss Chard

Sea Salt & Black Pepper

Water

Flaxseeds

Coconut Oil

Vanilla Vegan Powder

Baking Powder

Carrot

Avocado

Poppy seeds

Lemon juice

Ginger

Strawberries

Stevia

Coconut flakes

Paprika

Blueberries

Banana

Almond milk

Chia seeds

Lentils

Tomatoes

Okra

Broccoli

Week 2 shopping list

Sage Leaves

Cloves Garlic

Onion

Olive Oil

Red Potatoes

Black Beans

Parsley

Swiss Chard

Sea Salt & Black Pepper

Water

Flaxseeds

Coconut Oil

Vanilla Vegan Powder

Baking Powder

Carrot

Avocado

Poppy seeds

Lemon juice

Ginger

Strawberries

Stevia

Coconut flakes

Paprika

Blueberries

Banana

Almond milk

Chia seeds

Lentils

Tomatoes

Okra

Broccoli

Week 3 shopping list

Sage Leaves

Cloves Garlic

Onion

Olive Oil

Red Potatoes

Black Beans

Parsley

Swiss Chard

Sea Salt & Black Pepper

Water

Flaxseeds

Coconut Oil

Vanilla Vegan Powder

Baking Powder

Carrot

Avocado

Poppy seeds

Lemon juice

Ginger

Strawberries

Stevia

Coconut flakes

Paprika

Blueberries

Banana

Almond milk

Chia seeds

Lentils

Tomatoes

Okra

Broccoli

Week 4 shopping list

Sage Leaves

Cloves Garlic

Onion

Olive Oil

Red Potatoes

Black Beans

Parsley

Swiss Chard

Sea Salt & Black Pepper

Water

Flaxseeds

Coconut Oil

Vanilla Vegan Powder

Baking Powder

Carrot

Avocado

Poppy seeds

Lemon juice

Ginger

Strawberries

Stevia

Coconut flakes

Paprika

Blueberries

Banana

Almond milk

Chia seeds

Lentils

Tomatoes

Okra

Broccoli

Chapter 6: Continuing Plant Based Lifestyle

Steps to a healthy lifestyle

Start slow

Select a few plant-based foods and start with them through in one week. Begin with plant-based meals you enjoy eating, like oatmeal, jacket potatoes, pasta primavera, rice burrito, veggie stir-fry, three-bean chili, or lentil stew. However, you should then build based on these foods. We as humans are known to be creatures of habit; therefore we are likely going to settle for fewer varieties of dishes, therefore begin slowly and study this modern language of food with little or no pressure to be perfect.

Reduce meat and the consumption of processed food

Rather than going cold turkey from the start, begin by re-placing the amount of animal and plant-based foods you consume. It wil assist your body and mind with time to adapt to a new diet plan. Make less complex changes like including a large amount of fresh fruit or salad to your everyday meals. Next, avoid the consumption of dairy products and meat you don't like much anyway. After doing that, gradually work on trading animal-based ingredients for plant-based alternatives. For instance, if like eating beef chili, replace meat with portobello mushrooms or dried bulgur. Or, if you love eating tacos, choose plant-based options, such as Quinoa Taco Meat recipe and Mexican Spiced Cauliflower Tacos.

Settle for plant-based breakfast

The next step is for you to commit yourself to eat a minimum of one plant-based meal daily. A healthy vegetarian breakfast is a great place to begin. Foods like muffins, waffles, toasts, parfaits, pancakes, and smoothie bowls are great to start with. After that, you should work on vegetarianizing your meals.

Watch your protein

The average protein the body need is about 1gram for each kilogram of the body weight, a lot of people consume more than enough to acquire more. However, it's important to note that something is good doesn't guarantee that more is better. The excessive intake of protein is not just unnecessary, but it can also be dangerous to the health. You don't have to consume protein; what the body needs is for you to meet the requirements for the 9 essential amino acids that the body cannot synthesize by itself. Plant foods have amino acids in various quantities, and it contains enough protein to keep up with the requirements. It will not be possible to become deficient in protein in as much as you are taking in adequate calories to maintain the body and you are focusing on the consumption of whole foods and no refined foods.

Know your food

You can drink Diet Coke and decide that you are a vegan. Having knowledge of ways to ensure that your meal tastes delicious while still being wholesome and healthy is very important. A lot of commercial products, such as faux cheese and meat, are extremely processed and have the same nutrients that can be found in animal foods and this makes them very dangerous to health. However, these products are mostly packed with refined oils, salts, sugar, and flour. Thus, it is advisable to consume these kinds of foods occasionally. However, it's better to settle for whole foods as much as possible. Educate yourself based on nutrition and ways to make varieties of ingredients, or you can decide to pay a plant-based dietitian to guide you on the basics of transitioning to a plant-based diet.

Live on healthy foods

There are varieties of great products currently on the market, and it's easier to add foods that are plant-based to your diet. From dairy-free milk and kale chips to tofu and tempeh — there's always something available for every budget and palate. Therefore, calmly explore fresh produce and vegetarian aisles at your local stores. Fill your store with nutritious, plant-based products and store healthy snacks inaccessible areas such as your bag, kitchen counter, desk drawer, fridge and kitchen counter.

Make your meals exciting

Place emphasis on foods you love, which can be easily accessible by you. If you are not well skilled in the kitchen, then you go for more effortless recipes. For example, throw together frozen veggies and canned beans in a pan, include sauce, and cook to get tasty pot of soup. Next, you should study new steps to make our simple recipes a lot flavorful and fun.

Tips to stay on track

Don't forget to exercise

It has always been said that dieting is an effective way to lose weight. However, to keep the weight off, exercise is required. Many studies have shown that exercising while dieting is actually the best way to lose weight. Firstly, the diet becomes more effective and you lose weight faster if you exercise. But it also gets you in the habit of continuing your exercise when your diet is complete.

The exercise expected is not something that is not achievable either. Even with just forty-five minutes of exercise each day, can increase your weight loss by over ten percent! Anything that can get your heartbeat pulsing higher and faster than normal is considered exercise.

Often times, dieting will make you lose weight in many parts that you don't want to lose weight in, such as curvaceous or softening ones. Studies have shown that combined with exercise, dieting can help reduce your body mass index, waist circumference, and percentage of body fat.

Another concern is that with dieting, often times you appear lighter because your muscle and bone density is reduced. That is not a healthy lifestyle in the long term. Exercising will stimulate the growth of your muscles and have your body burn the fat instead of your metabolic tissues.

It is also important to understand that the idea behind dieting is that most people want to look skinnier and overall better.

However, lean is what will make you look perfect! Being lean will highlight your figure and keep your body healthy and toned. Skinny means that you have lost a lot of muscle density and water retention. In the long run, it can affect your calcium, iron, and zinc levels in your body.

Kick-starting your weight-loss journey

To get things done the right way and to ensure your body benefit from this diet, it is essential to consider the following things prio to starting this regimen.

Well Organized Meal plan

Please note that the main purpose of this book and diet plan is to help you lose weight and help in maintaining a healthy lifestyle. Because of this, you have to follow a strict plan to achieve your goals. This book provides a 21-day plant-based plan to kick-start your wellness journey. Please remember that this meal plan will require some commitment, and it is not how your diet will alway be structured after the 21-day plan. After 21 days, once your bod has adjusted, you will be able to make a consistent meal plan schedule where fasting is not required.

Understand Your Body

Getting your blood tested for the existence of any underlying condition is important to ensure that you start the regimen without worrying about it affecting your health negatively. Though, it doesn't harm your body, but in case you are suffering from a serious condition, it is best that you don't go on any sort of weight loss diet.

t is important to get your blood tested for lipid panel, liver and kidney function, inflammatory markers, thyroid panel and blood count.

Get enough sleep and relax efficiently

t is important that you understand that you must take this diet easy and relax while practicing it. Your goal must not be to quickly cut down your carb intake, so you can lose an enormous amount of your body weight as soon as possible. I suggest looking for maple sugar, date sugar, or even cane sugar. On top of these options, you can always choose pure maple syrup. The goal is to make sure that you're getting real maple syrup and not something that is maple-flavored.

Rather, you should reduce it slowly and gradually. Don't worry; you will still benefit a lot from this plan. Going easy on yourself helps you experience less side effects and enables your body to adjust comfortably to the completely new diet plan.

Get Professional Support

t is wise to get the assistance of a professional healthcare practitioner, dietician, or nutritionist who can help you out in preparing good meal plans for you. In this case, this e-book will do this job for you by providing you with more meal plans and guidance in the next series. Nonetheless, it is a good idea to consult a professional at least once before commencing the diet just to make sure that you know your body is ready for it. You will also find it easier to prepare good meal plans that are customized just for you.

n case, you suffer from heart diseases or other conditions such as epilepsy, HBP, diabetes (TYPE 2), Alzheimer's or any other medical condition, then it is absolutely essential for you to get a professional's help before and during the plan.

Create time

This is one of the most crucial factors to consider before implementing the low-carb diet. You must not start it when you are going through an extremely hectic schedule and have no time to spare for yourself. This is because this diet demands you to prepare special meals and get used to different foods that you aren't accustomed to eating regularly. These changes will stress you out, so you need to have enough time to devote to this new routine, at least for about two weeks.

Therefore, you must start the plant-based diet when you are emotionally, psychologically, and physically relaxed and free.

Be careful with other people's opinions

If you are to achieve optimal this goal, you will definitely need to understand that you cannot just eat anything even when in social places otherwise you will end up jeopardizing your entire regime since it takes time for any carbs you take to be completely out of your body. I suggest looking for maple sugar, date sugar, or even cane sugar. On top of these options, you can always choose pure maple syrup. The goal is to make sure that you're getting real maple syrup and not something that is maple-flavored.

As such, you should be psychologically prepared to take different foods that might attract some attention and well-meaning but often misleading comments about the diet. Being prepared will ensure you don't give up.

What you have to know about protein

Your decision to start a plant-based diet means that you need to more closely monitor the balance of nutrients, and especially protein, in your diet.

Eating enough protein can be ignored until it becomes a health issue.

Protein intake is the main problem of many who want to switch to a plant-based diet. The primary function of proteins is to maintain and build the body tissue.

Protein requirements for average adults can vary from 0.8 to 1.2 g per kilogram of body weight daily.

This protein should be complete, that is, its molecular structure should include all 8 basic proteins: valine, leucine, isoleucine, threonine, methionine, phenylalanine, tryptophan, lysine. The absence or insufficient amount of essential amino acids leads to growth retardation, weight loss, metabolic disorders, and in acute insufficiency - to death.

It is necessary to observe the principle of complementarity (mutual complement) of vegetable proteins. This principle implies the intake of two or three different types of plant foods, each of which partially contains different essential amino acids. Amino acids that are not present in one source of vegetable protein can be obtained from another. As a result of a combination of various sources of vegetable protein, we get the so-called complementary protein.

For example, breakfast consisting of lentil soup and wholemeal bread contains complementary amino acids that provide for the formation of a complete protein. Other examples are rice and beans, corn porridge or cornbread, and stewed beans.

Mistakes to avoid

Soup stock

You might be in need of a great stock to get your cooking going. However, you should be careful of some of the stocks on your kitchen shelves because they sometimes contain little amounts of animal fat or some other animal traces. Therefore, it's advisable to make use of self-made stocks that can be produced from leftover veggie scraps, herbs sprinkled in water, or sea vegetables. If you can't manufacture soup stock on your own, then go for products that clearly indicate "no animal-derived ingredients."

Bread

Plant-based eaters get disappointed after finding out that bread is a no go for them. Lots of common national brands make use of non-plant-based ingredients when making bread. Lots of whole-wheat breads are produced with milk products, for instance, there happen to be fewer traditional Italian breads that consist of

ard. But better supermarkets sell bread made from a local
bakery. Make sure to check the ingredients, however, locally
baked bread is usually plant-based. However, it is quite odd
because the local breads are mostly stored in a separate aisle
from the national brands. Therefore, purchase bread which are
manufactured from only whole grains and contain active cultures
or other ingredients like seeds, legumes or even nuts.

Veggie burgers or sausages

It might seem quite unreal to knowing that "veggie" burgers
sometimes contain non-plant-based ingredients in them. This is
why you should be very alert when reading labels. Lots of sausage
brands are made with little quantities of milk or eggs. Therefore,
you need to search for brands that are produced from organic soy
(not isolated soy protein because it is drastically processed),
whole grains, nuts, and seeds, or tempeh, with just herbs and
veggies included.

Pasta

Most kinds of pasta being sold in stores or restaurants are
produced with eggs included, this is normal because traditionally
made pasta produced with eggs included as one of its recipes.
However, the majority of dried kinds of pasta, which are gluten-
free and whole-grain, are recommended for people practicing a
plant-based diet; this is because this kind of pasta is produced
with 100 percent whole grain and water.

Dairy-Free Cheese

Although you might have heard that nuts, rice-based "cheeses"
and soy are non-dairy, they usually comprise some form of whey
protein or casein. However, to ensure safety, go for products that

indicate "vegan," this means that they are truly dairy-free. Alway read all the ingredients, look for words such as evaporated milk powder, casein, or rennet.

Granola

Granola is basically made with a mixture of dried fruits, raw grains, seeds, and nuts, that are mixed with a sweetener and either oil or butter. No rule of thumb can be used to figure out which granolas make use of which fats. In short, if you find yourself at a resort, restaurant or buffet, there's no way you can figure out where youFVr granola is sourced from or what it's made of. Therefore, it is always available to make them yourself.

Plant-based Diet Should be Balanced

For a plant-based diet to be good for health, it must be balanced.

The main issue if you are on any kind of restrictive eating regimen, is to make sure you are balancing the optimal amounts of protein fats and fiber on your plate at each meal.

If you are worried about having to find new foods to fill up your plate, now that so many edibles will disappear off your shopping list, this is a quick read of how easy it is to find healthy food once you decide to start a plant-based diet. There are more than enough plant food sources and produce very easily available, especially if you eat seasonally.

Chapter 7: Plant based meal prep

Benefits of meal prepping

There are many benefits to meal prepping or preparing meals in advance.

Here are some of them:

Saves time and effort – When you do meal prepping, you will only have to set aside a few hours of a day to organize your menu, shop for your ingredients, prepare, cook and store the dishes in the refrigerator or freezer. Cooking in bulk obviously saves time and effort come meal time as you will only have to reheat the dish and serve.

Saves money – Yes, you heard it right. This can definitely help you save money. How? Here's a fact, more than half of the adult population dedicate a big amount of their money to eating in restaurants and availing food delivery services. That's because they do not have any food prepared at home. This can be avoided by preparing meals in advance so that even if you're busy, you'll still have healthy and delicious foods that you can serve at home.

Helps you achieve better health – Preparing meals in advance helps make sure that you are on the right track in your diet. This results in better health, less risk of disease and so on.

Storage, heating and food safety

Setup your kitchen and tools

To succeed and make yourself accountable, you have to shape your environment to match your goals—starting with what you bring into your kitchen and put into your body. If you make sure you have a variety of healthy foods in your kitchen, you can always pull together a balanced meal. Even if you don't have exactly what a specific recipe calls for, you should have the components you need for substitutions. Let's give your kitchen a makeover.

The Pantry

Let's toss the refined flours, sugars, and oils, and opt instead for wholesome, unrefined versions. Stock up on whole grains, beans and legumes, and dried fruit.

•Whole grains (brown rice, quinoa, buckwheat, millet)

•Beans and legumes (chickpeas, kidney beans, lentils)

•Dried fruit (raisins, dates, dried apricots, cranberries)

•Unrefined oils (olive, coconut, toasted sesame)

•Vinegars (apple cider, balsamic, wine)

•Whole-grain flours (whole wheat, spelt, oat, buckwheat)

- Unrefined sweeteners (whole unrefined cane sugar like sucanat, coconut sugar, maple syrup, molasses, pure stevia)

- Sea salt

- Spices (ginger, cumin, coriander, turmeric, paprika, cinnamon)

- Dried herbs (basil, oregano, thyme, dill, herb mixes)

- Nutritional yeast

The Refrigerator

Let's toss the meats, cheeses, milk, eggs, and packaged meals. Stock up on fresh produce, nuts and seeds, and non-dairy choices.

- Leafy greens (lettuce, kale, chard, spinach)

- Fresh herbs and spices (parsley, basil, mint, garlic, ginger)

- Green/non-starchy vegetables (cucumber, bell peppers, green beans, broccoli, mushrooms)

- Starchy vegetables (carrots, beets, sweet potato, winter squash)

- Onions (sweet, red, yellow, green)

- Fruit (apples, oranges, plums, grapes, melon)

- Nuts and seeds (almonds, pecans, sunflower seeds, chia seeds, flaxseed)

- Nut and seed butters (peanut, almond, cashew, sunflower)

- Non-dairy milk (almond, soy)

The Freezer

Time to ditch the TV dinners, French fries, frozen waffles, ice cream, frozen pies, and cakes. Stock up on fresh-frozen produce and homemade stuff.

•Frozen berries, mango, melon

•Frozen ripe bananas for smoothies and creamy sorbet

•Frozen edamame beans, peas, corn, broccoli, spinach, and other fresh-frozen whole vegetables

•Food you cook in big batches and freeze in single servings (soups, stews, chili, tomato sauce, veggie burgers)

•Healthy desserts (whole-food brownies, muffins, cookies, fruit pies)

PLANT-BASED FAST FOOD AT HOME

Sometimes we don't have time to follow recipes. For those days, I've made you a sketch outline of a balanced meal, so you can throw it together with whatever happens to be in your kitchen.

Smoothie Builder

Build a perfect nourishing smoothie to start your day and fuel you to lunch. You'll need:

•Cup and straw: sipping from a reusable straw minimizes contact with your teeth for better dental health, and using an insulated cup or travel mug keeps your smoothie cool through the morning.

•Creaminess: banana (frozen makes it like ice cream), avocado, nut butter or non-dairy milk.

Omega-3s: 1 tablespoon flax or chia seeds.

Protein: a handful of rolled oats or quinoa flakes, or a scoop of plant-based protein powder.

Fruit: about 1 cup of berries, melon, grapes, cherries, apple, whatever you like.

Vegetable boost: greens such as spinach, sprouts, or kale; vegetables such as cucumber or carrots; fresh herbs such as mint or basil.

Superfood boost: fresh ginger, greens powder, matcha powder, probiotics, goji berries or powder, cocoa nibs.

Basics

There is no portion control, no carb counting and no calorie counting with this diet plan. You can eat when you're hungry, and you can eat until you get full. Simply make sure that you choose food from the right categories. Of course, there are going to be exceptions that you'll need to make occasionally. You need to be sure that you aren't eating too often from your sparingly food category for example.

Choose the One for You

You can choose the plant-based diet for you! Here are some of the most common plant-based diets out there.

grains, vegetables, nuts and seeds, but you'll not be able to eat any food that's sourced from animals.

Raw Veganism: This is a diet that includes uncooked and some dehydrated foods.

Vegetarianism: This is a diet that consists of legumes, vegetables, nuts and fruit. You can include eggs and dairy in this diet, but you aren't allowed meat.

Fruitarianism: This is a vegan diet that primarily involves fruit, but you should not use this if you are diabetic.

Ovo-lacto Vegetarianism: This encourages that you eat eggs and dairy along with your fruit and vegetables.

Ovo Vegetarianism: This is where you are allowed to eat eggs with your fruits and vegetables, but you still can't have dairy.

Lacto Vegetarianism: This allows you to have dairy but no eggs with your fruits and vegetables.

Semi-Vegetarianism: This is a mostly vegetarian diet with the occasional time that you can have meat.

Pescatarian: This is a semi-vegetarian diet that allows you to have dairy, eggs, shellfish and fish.

Macrobiotic Diet: This diet highlights whole grains, beans, miso soup, sea vegetables, vegetables, and naturally processed foods. This can be done with or without seafood and other anima products.

Grain

Whole grains contain complex carbohydrates for sustained energy and are a source of fiber, protein, vitamins (especially the B vitamins and vitamin E), minerals, essential fatty acids, and antioxidants. They are very difficult to digest raw so are generall cooked. Some have tough outer husks, while others have a shell with a soft whole grain inside. Always opt for whole grains, whic have all their nutrients intact, as opposed to white, refined, or polished grains, which are left with just the starch cells. There is an exciting array of whole grains available these days, with different textures and flavors. They include rice, millet, buckwheat, oats, quinoa, farro, barley, and amaranth.

Greens

Leafy vegetables or greens are some of the most healthy and nutritious foods. They contain many minerals (such as iron, magnesium and potassium) and vitamins (especially K, A, C and folate), as well as a lot of chlorophyll. A wide variety of leaves includes lettuce, spinach, cilantro, parsley, basil, green onions, chard, arugula, mustard greens, watercress, endive, escarole, sorrel etc.

Legumes

Legumes are plants that bear their fruit in pods; typically, we eat the fruit or seed. They are an important source of the amino acid lysine, are rich in fiber, vitamins, and minerals, and are low in fat. They are a healthier protein than animal products, as well as a cheaper one per gram of protein. The most well-known legumes are peas, beans, lentils, peanuts, and alfalfa.

Bowls

Build a perfect bowl for lunch or dinner that gives you all the nutrients and fuel you need for the rest of the day. You'll need:

Bowl: get a couple that are the same size to keep your portions consistent.

Leafy greens: grab a handful or two, as much as you want, of lettuce, arugula, spinach, kale, chard, parsley, or other greens.

•Starchy vegetables and/or whole grains: about 1 cup of sweet potato, winter squash, brown rice, quinoa, farro, soba noodles, rice noodles, and so on.

•Beans or legumes: about ½ cup of chickpeas, black beans, lentils, edamame, or other legumes.

•Other vegetables: about 1 cup of raw vegetables such as cucumber, bell pepper, tomato, and avocado; grilled such as zucchini, eggplant, and mushrooms; or steamed such as broccoli, carrots, and beets.

•Nuts or seeds: a small handful, either whole (pumpkin, cashews, almonds) or nut butter, which you can use as the base for the sauce.

•Sauce: a long, generous drizzle. Try the recipes in this book, like **Toasted Sesame Miso Dressing**, **Green Goddess Dressing**, or **Creamy Balsamic Dressing**, or check the ingredients to see if you can find a whole-foods variety in the store.

Chapter 8: Breakfast recipes

Chai Flavoured Quinoa

Total time: 35 minutes

Ingredients:

- ½ tbsp. Coconut Palm Sugar
- ½ cup Quinoa, washed
- 1 Chai Tea Bag
- 1 cup Almond Milk, unsweetened

Directions:

To begin with, mix the quinoa with the almond milk and chai tea bag in a small saucepan.

Heat it over a medium heat and bring the mixture to a boil.

Once it starts boiling, discard the chai bag.

Next, spoon in the coconut palm sugar and stir well.

Lower the heat and allow it to simmer for 18 to 20 minutes while keeping it covered.

Remove the saucepan from the heat. Set it aside for 10 minutes so that the quinoa absorbs all the liquid.

Finally, transfer the mixture to a serving bowl.

Serve immediately.

Spinach Tofu Scramble

Total time: 15 minutes

Ingredients:

- 2 tbsp. Olive Oil
- 1 tsp. Lemon Juice, freshly squeezed
- 2 Tomatoes, finely chopped
- ½ tsp. Soy Sauce
- 2 Garlic cloves, minced
- Salt & Pepper, as needed
- ¾ cup Mushrooms, finely sliced
- 1 lb. Tofu, extra-firm & crumbled
- 10 oz. Spinach

Directions:

First, take a medium-sized skillet and heat it over a medium-high heat.

Once the skillet becomes hot, spoon in the oil.

Next, stir in the tomatoes, mushrooms, and garlic.

Cook them for 2 to 3 minutes or until softened.

Now, lower the heat to medium-low and spoon in the spinach, lemon juice, tofu, and soy sauce.

Mix well and cook for a further 8 minutes while stirring occasionally.

Then, check the seasoning and add salt and pepper as needed.

Serve it hot.

Chai Flavoured Quinoa

Total time: 25 minutes

Ingredients:

- ½ tbsp. Coconut Palm Sugar
- ½ cup Quinoa, washed
- 1 Chai Tea Bag
- 1 cup Almond Milk, unsweetened

Directions:

To begin with, mix the quinoa with the almond milk and chai tea bag in a small saucepan.

Heat it over a medium heat and bring the mixture to a boil.

Once it starts boiling, discard the chai bag.

Next, spoon in the coconut palm sugar and stir well.

Lower the heat and allow it to simmer for 18 to 20 minutes while keeping it covered.

Remove the saucepan from the heat. Set it aside for 10 minutes so that the quinoa absorbs all the liquid.

Finally, transfer the mixture to a serving bowl.

Serve immediately.

Cauliflower Porridge

Total time: 25 minutes

Ingredients:

- ½ of 1 Banana, ripe
- ½ tsp. Vanilla Extract
- 2 cups Cauliflower Extract
- 1 ¼ tsp. Cinnamon
- 1 cup Soy Milk, unsweetened
- 2 tsp. Maple Syrup
- ¼ of 1 Pear
- ½ tbsp. Almond Butter
- 4 Strawberries
- 1/8 tsp. Salt

Directions:

To make this nutritious oatmeal, place the cauliflower in the food processor and process until the cauliflower becomes riced or is in small granules.

Stir in the banana and mash it well.

After that, place the riced cauliflower- banana mixture into a small saucepan.

Heat the mixture over a medium-high heat.

Next, spoon in all the remaining ingredients into the saucepan and give a good stir.

Lower the heat and cook for 14 minutes. Continue cooking until ready.

Place the oatmeal into a serving bowl and serve it immediately or warm.

Overnight Hemp Cereal

Total time: 6 hours 10 minutes

Ingredients:

- ¼ tsp. Cinnamon
- ¼ cup Rolled Oats
- 1 tbsp. Raisins
- 3 tbsp. Hemp Seeds
- ½ cup Soy Milk, unsweetened
- 3 tbsp. Hemp Seeds
- 1 tbsp. Maple Syrup

Directions:

First, add all the ingredients to a large mason jar and mix well.

Now, place them in the refrigerator overnight.

Serve in the morning and enjoy.

Overnight Chia Oatmeal

Total time: 20 minutes

Ingredients:

- ¾ cup Rolled Oats
- 1 cup Plant Milk
- 2 tbsp. Chia Seeds
- ½ cup Water
- 2 tbsp. Agave Syrup
- ½ tsp. Cinnamon
- 1 Banana, ripe & mashed
- Dash of Sea Salt
- 1 tsp. Vanilla
- 2 tbsp. Peanut Butter
- 1 ½ tbsp. Water

Directions:

To begin with, combine the chia seeds, sea salt, cinnamon, and oats in a mason jar until mixed well.

Next, pour in the hemp milk along with the banana, vanilla, and water to the jar. Stir again.

Now, mix the peanut butter with water in a small mixing bowl for 2 to 3 minutes. Tip: The mixture should be creamy in texture.

After that, pour the creamy mixture over the oats and stir.

Then, place the mason jar in the refrigerator overnight.

Add your favorite topping and enjoy.

Quinoa Oatmeal

Total time: 15 minutes

Ingredients:

- 2 Bananas, ripe
- ½ cup Quinoa, dry
- 2 tbsp. Peanut Butter, organic
- ¾ cup Almond Milk, light
- 1 tsp. Vanilla
- ½ tsp. Cinnamon, ground

Directions:

To start, place the quinoa, nutmeg, almond milk, cinnamon, and vanilla in a small saucepan.

Heat the saucepan over a medium heat and bring the mixture to a boil.

Once it starts boiling, lower the heat and allow it to simmer for 10 to 15 minutes. Tip: The quinoa should have absorbed all the liquid in this time.

Next, fluff the quinoa mixture with a fork and then transfer to a serving bowl.

Now, spoon in the peanut butter and stir well.

Finally, top with the banana.

Lunch and Dinner Recipes

Three Bean Pasta

Total time: 60 minutes

Ingredients:

- 1 tbsp. Olive Oil
- 1 tsp. Oregano, dried
- ½ cup Kidney Beans, cooked
- 15 oz. Tomatoes, chopped
- 1 Onion, large & sliced
- ½ cup Navy Beans
- Salt & Pepper, as needed
- 2 Garlic cloves, minced
- 4 tbsp. Nut Flour
- ½ cup Chickpeas, cooked
- 2 cups Soy Milk

- ½ tsp. Nutmeg, grated
- 1 ½ cup Spinach
- 1 cup Pasta tubes
- 2 tbsp. Vegan Butter

Directions:

For making this delightful pasta fare, you need to heat a large skillet over medium-high heat.

To this, spoon in the oil and then add onion, garlic, and pepper.

Cook them for 6 to 8 minutes or until softened.

Then add beans, oregano, tomatoes, and chickpeas to it.

Now, check for seasoning and add salt and pepper as needed.

Next, cover the saucepan and allow it to simmer for 18 to 20 minutes.

Meanwhile, cook the pasta by following the manufacturer's instructions given in the packet.

Once pasta is cooked, mix it with the bean mixture well.

Meanwhile, to make the sauce, heat the vegan butter in a saucepan over medium heat.

When it melts, spoon in the flour and pour the soy milk.

Now, bring the flour mixture to a simmer and cook for 3 minutes while stirring it continuously.

Add nutmeg, salt, and pepper to it. Cook the spinach for 2 minutes or until wilted. Add to the sauce.

Finally, pour the sauce over the cooked pasta bean mixture. Serve and enjoy.

Black Bean Wrap with Hummus

Total time: 35 minutes

Ingredients:

- 1 Poblano Pepper, roasted
- ½ packet of Spinach
- 1 Onion, chopped
- 2 Whole Grain Wraps
- ½ can of Black Beans
- 1 Bell Pepper, seeded & chopped
- 4 oz. Mushrooms, sliced
- ½ cup Corn
- 8 oz. Red Bell Pepper Hummus, roasted

Directions:

First, preheat the oven to 450 °F.

Next, spoon in oil to a heated skillet and stir in the onion.

Cook them for 2 to 3 minutes or until softened.

After that, stir in the bell pepper and saute for another 3 minutes.

Then, add mushrooms and corn to the skillet. Saute for 2 minutes.

In the meantime, spread the hummus over the wraps.

Now, place the sautéed vegetables, spinach, poblano strips, and beans.

Roll them into a burrito and place on a baking sheet with the seam side down.

Finally, bake them for 9 to 10 minutes.

Serve them warm.

Tofu Bean Salad

Total time: 40 minutes

Ingredients:

For the dressing:

- ¼ cup Tahini
- 1/8 tsp. Onion Powder
- ¼ cup Water
- ¼ tsp. Salt
- 1 Garlic clove, chopped
- ½ tsp. Parsley, fresh & chopped
- 1 tbsp. Lemon Juice
- For the Tofu:
- 1 tsp. Arrowroot Powder
- 1 block Tofu, firm
- 1 tsp. Worcestershire Sauce, vegan
- 1 tbsp. Soy Sauce
- For the salad:
- ½ cup White Beans
- ½ cup Red Beans
- ½ cup Chickpeas
- 1 cup Tomato, diced
- 2½ oz. Spring Mix
- ½ cup Yellow Bell Pepper, diced

Directions:

First, preheat the oven to 425 °F.

Place tofu cubes, arrowroot powder, Worcestershire sauce, and soy sauce in a large mixing bowl and mix well.

Toss well so that the tofu coats the sauce well.

Next, arrange the tofu cubes on a parchment paper-lined baking sheet.

Bake for 28 minutes or until the tofu are crispy.

Remove the sheet from the pan and allow it to cool.

In the meantime, to make the dressing, keep all the ingredients in the blender. Blend for 1 minute until you get a smooth sauce.

Finally, add all the salad ingredients to a large mixing bowl along with the baked tofu. Drizzle the dressing over it and toss.

Serve and enjoy.

Cauliflower Bowl

Total time: 40 minutes

Ingredients:

- 1 Sweet Potato, peeled & cubed
- 1 Avocado, mashed
- For the rice:
- 1 Cauliflower Head, torn into florets
- ½ tsp. Salt
- 1 tbsp. Avocado Oil
- 2 cloves of Garlic, minced
- ½ of 1 Onion, chopped finely
- For the black beans:
- 2 tbsp. Water
- ½ tbsp. Avocado Oil
- ½ tsp. Cumin Powder
- ½ of 1 Onion, chopped finely
- ½ tsp. Chilli Powder
- 14 oz. Black Beans
- Salt & Pepper, as needed
- 2 Chipotle Peppers in Adobo Sauce
- 1 tbsp. Tomato Paste

Directions:

To start with, place the cauliflower florets in a food processor and process them until they are riced & grainy.

After that, spoon in avocado oil to a heated skillet over medium-high heat.

Next, stir in the onion and saute them for 2 minutes or until softened.

Then, spoon in the garlic and cook for further one minute or until aromatic.

Now, add the riced cauliflower to the skillet and give a good stir until everything comes together.

Taste for seasoning. Add more salt if needed.

Once the cauliflower rice is ready, heat the avocado oil in a medium saucepan over medium-high heat.

Add the onion and bell pepper to it and cook for 2 to 3 minutes or until cooked.

Then, stir in the remaining ingredients for the beans into it and mix well. Cook for two more minutes.

Meanwhile, we also need to roast the sweet potato. For that, preheat the oven to 400 °F.

Now, arrange the sweet potato on a parchment paper-lined baking sheet and bake for 28 to 30 minutes or until tender. Flip halfway through

Finally, add cauliflower rice to the bottom of the serving plate and then top it with the beans and with roasted sweet potato.

Serve and enjoy.

Peanut Tofu Sauce Noodles

Total time: 25 minutes

Ingredients:

- 6 oz. Brown Rice Noodles
- ¼ tsp. Salt
- 2 ¼ cup Water
- 1 tsp. Lime Juice
- ½ cup Carrots, sliced
- 4 oz. Tofu, cubed
- 3 tbsp. Peanut Butter
- ½ of 1 Red Bell Pepper, sliced
- 1 tbsp. Sweetener of your choice
- 3 tsp. Sriracha
- 2 tbsp. Cilantro, fresh & chopped
- 2 tsp. Soy Sauce
- Pinch of Cayenne Pepper
- ½ tsp. White Vinegar
- ½ tsp. Garlic Powder
- ½ cup Celery, chopped
- 1 tbsp. Ginger, minced

Directions:

First, place the noodles and water in a large pot and heat it over medium-high heat.

The water should cover the noodles. Keep the veggies on the sides of the top.

Next, stir in all the remaining ingredients, excluding the cilantro and celery to the pot and give a stir.

Now, bring the veggie mixture to a boil while stirring it occasionally.

Once it starts boiling, add the celery and cook for another 2 to 3 minutes.

Then, taste for seasoning and add more salt and pepper as needed.

Finally, garnish it with cilantro and allow it to sit for a minute or two before serving.

Serve hot.

Quinoa Edamame Salad

Total time: 30 minutes

Ingredients:

- 1 cup Corn, frozen
- 1/8 tsp. Black Pepper, grounded
- 2 cups Edamame, shelled & frozen
- ¼ tsp. Chilli Powder
- 1 cup Quinoa, cooked & cooled
- 1 tbsp. Lime Juice, fresh
- 1 Green Onion, sliced
- ¼ tsp. Thyme, dried
- 2 tbsp. Cilantro, fresh & chopped
- 1/4 tsp. Salt
- ½ of 1 Red Bell Pepper, chopped
- 1 tbsp. Lemon Juice
- Pinch of Cayenne Pepper
- 1 ½ tbsp. Olive Oil

Directions:

Heat water in a large pot over medium heat.

To this, stir in the edamame and corn.

Boil them slightly and cook them until they are tender.

Once cooked, drain the water and set it aside.

Now, combine all the remaining veggies in a large bowl along with the cooked corn and edamame. Toss well.

In the meantime, to make the dressing, mix olive oil, lemon juice, lime juice, black pepper, thyme, chilli powder, and cayenne until emulsified.

Next, drizzle the dressing over the salad and place it in the refrigerator for at least 2 hours.

Serve and enjoy.

Bolognese Pasta

Total time: 35 minutes

Ingredients:

- 15 oz. Garbanzo Beans, drained, washed & dried
- ¼ cup Extra Virgin Olive Oil
- ¼ cup Parsley, fresh & chopped
- 1 Carrot, large & diced
- 24 oz. Marinara Sauce
- 1 Celery Stalk, large & diced
- 4 Garlic cloves, minced
- 8 oz. Pasta of your choice

- 1 Shallot, large & diced
- ¼ tsp. Black Pepper, grounded
- 1 tsp. Sea Salt
- 2 tsp. Maple Syrup
- ½ cup Oats Milk

Directions:

Heat oil in a large-sized saucepan over medium-high heat.

To this, stir in the carrot, celery, shallots, pepper, and salt.

Now, saute the veggies for 2 to 3 minutes or until softened.

Next, spoon in the garlic and cook for further 1 minute or until aromatic.

Then, place the garbanzo beans in the food processor and process them by pulsing them nine times.

After that, spoon in the processed garbanzo beans and marinara sauce to the saucepan. Mix well.

Once combined, pour the oats milk and maple syrup to it. Combine.

Cook for 5 minutes and then lower the heat.

Simmer the mixture for few minutes while keeping it covered with a lid.

Meanwhile, boil a pot of water over medium-high heat.

Add the pasta once the water starts boiling and cook by following the manufacturer's instructions. Cook until al dente.

Finally, stir in the cooked pasta to the sauce mixture and coat well.

Garnish with basil and parsley before serving.

Apple Lentil Salad

Total time: 30 minutes

Ingredients:

- 2 cups Lentil, dried
- ½ cup Pepitas, roasted
- 1 tsp. Salt
- 2 Celery Stalks, chopped
- 2 Apples, medium & chopped
- ¼ cup Cranberries, dried
- 1 tbsp. Rosemary, fresh & chopped
- 1 tbsp. Lemon Juice
- 2 tbsp. Parsley, chopped
- Dressing of your preference

Directions:

To start with, cook the lentils by following the instructions given in the packet until they are tender.

Once cooked, allow them to cool and place them in the refrigerator until used.

Next, mix the apples with lemon juice in a bowl. Keep it in the refrigerator.

After that, combine the chopped apples with the lentils and the remaining ingredients in the bowl.

Now, drizzle the dressing of your choice and place it in the refrigerator for at least an hour before serving.

Serve and enjoy.

Spaghetti with Chickpeas Meatballs

Total time: 45 minutes

Ingredients:

- 1/2 cup Breadcrumbs
- 1 tsp. Italian Seasoning
- 3 cups Chickpeas, drained & rinsed
- ½ tsp. Salt
- 3 tbsp. Flax Seed, grounded
- 2 tsp. Onion Powder
- 8 tbsp. Water
- ½ tbsp. Garlic Powder
- ¼ cup Nutritional Yeast
- For the pasta:
- 1 lb. Spaghetti
- 25 oz. Pasta Sauce

Directions:

First, preheat the oven to 325 °F.

After that, combine the flax seeds with water in a small bowl and set it aside for 5 minutes.

Next, place the chickpeas and salt in the food processor and process them for one minute or until you get a smooth mixture.

Now, transfer the chickpea mixture and the flaxseed mixture to a large mixing bowl. Stir well.

Once combined, add all the remaining ingredients needed to the bowl.

Give everything a good stir and mix well.

Then, make balls out of this mixture and arrange them on a parchment paper-lined baking sheet while leaving ample space in between.

Bake them for 33 to 35 minutes. Turn them once halfway through.

In the meantime, make the spaghetti by following the instructions given on the packet. Cook until al dente.

Finally, place the spaghetti on the serving plate and top it with the meatballs and pasta sauce.

Serve and enjoy.

Vegan Sloppy Joes

Total time: 30 minutes

Ingredients:

- 1½ cup Tomato Sauce
- 1 tbsp. Extra Virgin Olive Oil
- 1/8 tsp. Black Pepper, grounded
- 1/8 tsp. Cayenne Pepper
- 1 tsp. Sweet Paprika
- 2 Garlic cloves
- 2 tsp. Onion Powder
- ¼ of 1 Onion, chopped
- 2 tsp. Garlic Powder
- ½ of 1 Red Bell Pepper, chopped
- 1 tbsp. Cane Sugar
- ½ of 1 Green Bell Pepper, chopped
- 2 tbsp. Tomato Paste
- 15 oz. Lentils, cooked
- 2 tbsp. Soy Sauce
- 6 Whole Wheat Hamburgers

Directions:

To start with, heat a large skillet over medium-high heat.

Now, spoon in the oil and once the oil becomes hot, add the veggies and cayenne pepper.

Saute them for 6 minutes or until they are golden brown colored. Stir occasionally.

Next, stir in all the remaining ingredients to the skillet and cook them for 10 to 12 minutes or until the mixture is thickened.

Finally, take the buns and fill them with the filling.

Serve and enjoy.

Desserts Recipes

Easy Brownies

Total time: 25 minutes

Ingredients:

- 2 Tablespoons Coconut Oil, Melted
- ½ Cup Peanut Butter, Salted
- ¼ Cup Warm Water
- 2 Cups Dates, Pitted
- 1/3 Cup Dark Chocolate chips
- 1/3 Cup Cocoa Powder
- ½ Cup Raw Walnuts, Chopped

Directions:

Heat the oven to 350, and then get out a loaf pan. Place parchment paper in it, and then get out a food processor. Blend your dates until it's a fine mixture. Add in some hot water, and blend well until the mixture become an as smooth batter.

Add in the coconut oil, cacao powder, and peanut butter. Blend more, and then fold in the chocolate and walnuts. Spread this into your loaf pan.

Bake for fifteen minutes, and then chill before serving.

Butterscotch Tart

Total time: 50 minutes

Ingredients:

Crust:

- ½ Cup Sugar
- ¼ Cup Coconut Oil
- 1 Teaspoon Vanilla Extract, Pure
- ½ Teaspoon Sea Salt
- 2 Cups Almond Meal Flour

Filling:

- 2/3 Cup Light Brown Sugar, Packed
- 1 Teaspoon Kosher Salt
- ½ Cup Coconut Oil
- 2/3 Cup Coconut Cream, Canned
- Flaked Sea Salt, As Needed
- 1 Green Apple, Sliced

Directions:

Turn the oven to 375, and then get out a bowl. Prepare your crust ingredients by mixing everything until smooth. Spread this into a tart pan that's nine inches. Spread it as evenly as possible. Freeze for ten minutes, and then bake for fifteen. It should be golden brown.

Prepare the filling by cooking it al in a saucepan for twenty-five minutes. It should thicken and allow it to cool. You will need to stir often to keep it from burning.

Add this to the tart, and then chill for two hours before serving.

Lemon Cake

Total time: 5 hours 10 minutes

Ingredients:

Crust:

- 1 Cup Dates, Pitted
- 2 Tablespoons Maple Syrup
- 2 ½ Cups Pecans

Filling:

- 1 Lemon, Juiced & Zested
- ¾ Cup Maple Syrup
- 1 ½ Cups Pineapple, Crushed
- 3 Cups Cauliflower Rice, Prepared
- 3 Avocados, Halved & Pitted
- ½ Teaspoon Vanilla Extract, Pure
- ½ Teaspoon Lemon Extract
- 1 Pinch Cinnamon

Topping:

- 1 Teaspoon Vanilla Extract, Pure
- 1 ½ Cups Coconut Yogurt, Plain
- 3 Tablespoons Maple Syrup

Directions:

Get a nine-inch springform pan out, lining it with parchment paper.

Put your pecans in a food processor, grinding until fine. Stir in the maple syrup and dates, blending for a minute more. Spread this into your pan to make the crust.

Blend your maple syrup, pineapple, lemon juice, lemon zest, cauliflower rice, and avocados in a food processor. Add in the lemon extract, cinnamon, and vanilla. Mix well.

Top your crust with this mixture, and freeze for five hours.

To make your topping whisk all ingredients together, spreading it over your prepared cake.

Spice Cake

Total time: 50 minutes

Ingredients:

- 1 Sweet Potato, Cooked & Peeled
- ½ Cup Applesauce, Unsweetened
- ½ Cup Almond Milk
- ¼ Cup Maple Syrup, Pure
- 1 Teaspoon Vanilla Extract, Pure
- 2 Cups Whole Wheat Flour
- ½ Teaspoon Ground Cinnamon
- ½ Teaspoon Baking Soda
- ¼ Teaspoon Ground Ginger

Directions:

Turn your oven to 350, and then get a large bowl out. Mash your sweet potatoes and then mix in the vanilla, milk, and maple syrup. Mix well.

Stir in the baking soda, cinnamon, flour, and ginger. Mix well.

Pour this batter into a baking dish that's been lined with parchment paper. Bake the batter for forty-five minutes.

Allow it to cool before slicing to serve.

Avocado Blueberry Cheesecake

Total time: 2 hours 20 minutes

Ingredients:

Crust:

- 1 Cup Rolled Oats
- 1 Cup Walnuts
- 1 Teaspoon Lime Zest
- 1 Cup Soft Pitted Dates

Filling:

- 2 Tablespoons Maple Syrup
- 1 Cup Blueberries, Frozen
- 2 Avocados, Peeled & Pitted
- 2 Tablespoons Basil, Fresh & Minced Fine
- 4 Tablespoons Lime Juice

Directions:

Pulse all crust ingredients together in your food processor, and then press into a pie pan.

Blend all filling ingredients until smooth, and pour it into the crust. Smooth out and freeze for two hours before serving.

Mango Cream Pie

Total time: 50 minutes

Ingredients:

Crust:

- ½ Cup Rolled Oats
- 1 Cup Cashews
- 1 Cup Dates, Pitted

Filling:

- 2 Mangos, Large, Peeled & Chopped
- ½ Cup Water
- 1 Cup Coconut Milk, Canned
- ½ Cup Coconut, Shredded & Unsweetened

Directions:

Get out a food processor and pulse all of your crust ingredients together. Press into an eight-inch pie pan.

Blend all filling ingredients. It should be thick and make sure it's smooth.

Pour it into the crust, and smooth out. Allow it to set in the freezer for thirty minutes.

Allow it to come to room temperature for ten to fifteen minutes before slicing.

Coconut Chia Pudding

Total time: 30 minutes

Ingredients:

- 1 Lime, Juiced & Zested
- 14 Ounces Coconut Milk, Canned
- 2 Dates
- 2 Tablespoons Chia Seeds, Ground
- 2 Teaspoons Matcha Powder

Directions:

Get out a blender and blend everything until smooth. Chill for twenty minutes before serving.

Chocolate Banana Cupcakes

Total time: 45 minutes

Ingredients:

- 3 Bananas
- 1 Cup Almond Milk
- 2 Tablespoons Almond Butter
- ¼ Cup Chia Seeds
- 1 Teaspoon Apple Cider Vinegar
- 1 Teaspoon Vanilla Extract, Pure
- 1 ¼ Cups Whole Grain Flour
- ½ Cup Rolled Oats
- ¼ Cup Coconut Sugar
- ½ Teaspoon Baking Soda
- 1 Teaspoon Baking Powder
- Pinch Sea Salt
- ¼ Cup Dark Chocolate Chips
- ½ Cup Cocoa Powder, Unsweetened

Directions:

Heat the oven to 350, and get out a muffin pan. Grease it. Place your almond butter, vinegar, milk, bananas, and vanilla together. Puree until smooth.

Place the flour, sugar, oats, baking soda, baking powder, chia seeds, cocoa powder, chocolate chips, and salt together in a bowl. Mix well.

Mix your wet and dry ingredients, and make sure there are no lumps.

Spoon into muffin cups and bake for twenty to twenty-five minutes.

Allow them to cool before serving. They should be moist.

Snacks

Dark Chocolate Hemp Energy Bites

Total time: 20 minutes

Ingredients

- 1 cup of oats (rolled)
- ½ cup of butter (almond)
- ¼ cup of hemp seeds
- 3 tbsp of maple syrup
- 3 tbsp of mini chocolate chips
- A pinch of salt
- 3 tbsp of coconut flakes (unsweetened)

Directions

1.In a medium container, mix all the ingredients and blend.

2. Take1 tbsp of dough and shape it into a ball.

3. Position the ball on a baking tray pierced and repeat once all 1 balls

are rolled out.

4. Firm up in the refrigerator for a few hours in the refrigerator and serve afterwards.

No- Bake Vegan Protein Bar

Total time: 5 minutes

Ingredients

- 3 cups of rolled oats (gluten- free)
- 4 scoops of protein powder of your choice
- 1 cup of almond butter (smooth)
- 1 cup of maple syrup
- 1 tbsp of water
- 1 cup of chocolate chips

Directions

Line a 10 x 10-inch plate with baking sheet.

Add your rolled oats with protein powder to a large bowl and mix well. Set aside.

Combine the almond butter with the maple syrup in a small pot and melt over low heat with continuous stirring.

Mix both wet and dry ingredients, fold in the chocolate chips and spread the mixture on the baking sheet.

4. Refrigerate for at least 2 hours until the batter firms up.

Remove from the fridge, cut into squares and enjoy.

Chocolate Peanut Butter Banana Shake

Total time: 5 minutes

Ingredients

- 1/4 cup of peanut butter (creamy)2 pcs of bananas (frozen)
- ½ cup of milk
- ½ cup of vanilla Greek yogurt (low fat)
- 2 tbsp of cocoa (powder)
- 3/4 cup of ice

Directions

Put all the ingredients in the blender.

Pulse on high until smooth texture forms.

Pour into serving glasses and enjoy immediately.

Black Bean Chocolate Orange Mousse

Total time: 25 minutes

Ingredients

- ½ oz of dates (pitted)

15oz of black beans (rinsed, drained)

8 tbsp of maple syrup

5 tbsp of cacao powder (raw)

- 2 tbsp of coconut oil (melted)

- 4 tbsp of milk (non-dairy)

- 1 organic orange (zest)

- 1 tsp of cacao nibs (raw, optional)

Directions

Blend the dates and black beans in a food processor until smoothly mixed, 1 minute.

Incorporate the maple syrup, milk, cocoa powder, coconut oil, and orange zest into the mixture until well combined.

Divide the mixture into 5 to 6 cups, top with the nibs of cacao and a bit of extra zest of orange.

Cool in the fridge for 1 hour before serving.

Raspberry Black Bean Brownies

Total time: 15 minutes

Ingredients

2 cups of black beans (drained, soaked)

2 chia eggs + 6 tbsp of water

½ cup of pure date sugar

4 tbsp of coconut oil

½ cup of cacao (powder)

pinch of baking powder

1/2 tsp of pink Himalayan salt

1 tsp of vanilla (powder)

1 cup of raspberries

handful of dark chocolate (chunks)

handful of pecans (chopped)

Directions

Set the oven to 350 F.

Combine all the ingredients up to the raspberries in a blender until well incorporated.

Grease a baking sheet with some oil and spread the mixture on top. Scatter the raspberries, chocolate chips, and pecans on top while pressing with a spoon to sit in the berries, chocolate, and pecans.

Bake the batter in the oven until set and toothpick inserted into the brownies come out clean, 10 to 15 minutes.

Remove from the oven, cut into square pieces and enjoy.

Easy Banana Cacao Ice Cream

Total time: 15 minutes

Ingredients

3 cups of cashew nuts

1/3 cup of water

a pinch of salt

½ cup of rolled oats

1 bean (vanilla)

1 large size banana (frozen, sliced)

handful of dates

Directions

Prepare the cashew first: immerse the cashews in a container.

Clean and flush. Blend with water and salt. Immerse the oats with the vanilla seeds extracted from the vanilla bean in a bowl a least one hour in advance.

Blend rolled oats, frozen banana slices, vanilla bean seeds, and cashew milk and pitted dates. Ready to serve!

Easy Banana Cacao Ice Cream

Total time: 15 minutes

Ingredients

2 tbsp of almond butter

4 pcs bananas (frozen, peeled)

/4 cup of cocoa (powder)

chocolate chunks/ chips (optional, topper)

Directions

Blend the almond butter, frozen bananas and cocoa powder over high speed while pushing the mixture down until smooth ice cream mixture forms.

Pour the mixture into a loaf pan, level the top, and freeze.

Scoop the ice cream into serving bowls, top with the chocolate chunks and enjoy!

Chocolate- Covered Black Bean Brownie Pops

Total time: 40 minutes

Ingredients

5 tbsp of raw cacao (powder)

5oz of black beans (drained, rinsed)

tbsp of maple syrup

1/8 tsp of sea salt (fine grain)

•2 tbsp of sunflower seed butter

•12 pcs of cake pops

•3/4 cup of chocolate chips (vegan)

Directions

Combine the cocoa powder, black beans, maple syrup, sea salt and sunflower butter in a food processor or blender. For a few minutes, pump and cycle until the mixture is well blended and pudgy.

Flour the mixture into twelve balls (about two tablespoons each per size) and place on a cake pop. Put in the fridge for 15-20 minutes to chill

Heat the chocolate in a microwave and when the brownie pops harden, coat each in the chocolate and serve.

Chocolate Black Bean Smoothie

Total time: 5 minutes

Ingredients

- 4 banana (frozen)
- 4 cup of cauliflower (frozen)
- 2 cup of beans (black)
- 4-8 medjool dates (pitted)
- 4 cups of almond milk
- 4 tbsp of hemp seeds
- 4 tbsp of cocoa powder
- 4 tsp of cinnamon (ground)

Directions

Put all the ingredients in the blender. Combine until the texture is smooth.

Pour into a glass and garnish with nibs of cocoa on top. Serve immediately.

Vegan Apricot and Date Truffles

Total time: 40 minutes

Ingredients

- 1 cup of medjool dates (organic, pitted)
- ½ cup of dried apricots (organic, pitted)
- 1 scoop of Protein Classic (Organic)
- 2 tbsp of coconut oil (organic)

- 2 tbsp of almond butter (organic)
- 2 tbsp of shredded coconut (organic, unsweetened)

2 tbsp of chia seeds (organic)

Directions

Add all the ingredients to a food processor or blender except for the shredded coconut and chia seeds and process until a well combined and crumbly, sticky texture forms.

Use your fingertips to grab a spoonful of the mixture, curl tightly into your fist and form into a ball shape.

In a plate with the coconut flakes and chia seeds, roll each truffle until well coated.

Arrange on a parchment-paper lined cookie sheet and refrigerate until firm, 15-30 minutes.

Remove from the oven and enjoy.

Smoothies and Drinks

Apple Cherry Smoothie

Total time: 10 minutes

Ingredients

- 1 cup cold cranberry juice

- ½ cup red cherries, pitted

  2 Honey Crisp apples, cored and chopped

  1 frozen banana, peeled

  ¼ cup ice cubes

Directions

Add all the ingredients to a blender and process until smooth.

Pour the smoothie into 4 glasses and enjoy immediately.

Avocado Banana Zinger

Total time: 10 minutes

Ingredients

- 1 large avocado, pitted and peeled

- 1 large frozen banana, peeled

- ½ cup unsweetened almond milk

- A small handful fresh mint leaves

Directions

Combine all the ingredients in a blender and process until smooth

Divide into 4 serving glasses, insert straws and enjoy immediately.

Coconut Chocolate Shake

Total time: 10 minutes

Ingredients

- 1 cup unsweetened coconut milk

- 2 frozen bananas, peeled

- 2 tbsp coconut cream

- 1 tbsp flaxseed meal

- 3 tbsp unsweetened cocoa powder

- 1 tsp vanilla extract

- 1/3 cup ice cubes

Directions

Pour all the ingredients into a blender and process until smooth.

Divide into 4 glasses and serve immediately.

Berry Merry Zinger

Total time: 10 minutes

Ingredients

- 1 cup water
- 1 cup frozen mixed berries of your choice
- 1 tsp coconut oil
- 1 large frozen banana, peeled
- 1 lime, juiced
- 1 tsp pure maple syrup

Directions

Process all the ingredients in a blender until smooth.

Pour the drink into 4 serving glasses and enjoy immediately!

Dandelion Mango Smoothie

Total time: 10 minutes

Ingredients

- 1 cup unsweetened soy milk
- 1 cup chopped sweet mango, frozen
- 2 cups dandelion greens
- 1 frozen ripe bananas, peeled

• ¼ cup frozen chopped pineapples

Directions

Pour all the ingredients into a blender and process until smooth.

Share the drink among 4 glasses and enjoy immediately.

Gingerbread Man Smoothie

Total time: 10 minutes

Ingredients

    1 cup unsweetened almond milk

    1 large frozen banana, peeled

    ½ tsp cinnamon powder

    1 tsp vanilla extract

    ¼ tsp ginger powder

    1 tbsp chia seeds

    2 tbsp maple syrup

    2 tbsp unsweetened coconut flakes for topping

Directions

1. Add all the ingredients to a blender except for the coconut flakes and process until smooth.

2. Pour the smoothie into 4 glasses, top with the coconut flakes and enjoy immediately!

Orange Papaya Smoothie

Total time: 10 minutes

Ingredients

- 1 cup chopped papaya pulp

- 1 cup fresh orange juice

- ¼ cup unsweetened almond milk

- 1 tbsp flax seeds

- 2 tbsp pure maple syrup

- ¼ cup ice cubes

Directions

Add all the ingredients to a blender and process until smooth.

Divide into serving glasses and enjoy immediately!

Minty Green Booster

Total time: 10 minutes

Ingredients

- 1 ½ cups hemp milk

- 1 large frozen banana, peeled

  2 handfuls chopped kale

- ¼ cup fresh mint leaves, stems removed

Directions

Combine all the ingredients in a blender and process until smooth.

Divide the drink into 4 glasses and enjoy immediately!

Blueberry Pear Shake

Total time: 10 minutes

Ingredients

- ½ cup frozen blueberries

- ¼ cup chopped frozen pears

- 1 cup unsweetened coconut milk + more as desired

- 2 tbsp coconut cream

- 1 tsp pure maple syrup

- ¼ tsp vanilla extract

- 12 ice cubes

Directions

Add all the ingredients to a blender and process until smooth.

Divide the smoothie into 4 glasses and enjoy immediately.

Chocolate Orange Smoothie

Total time: 10 minutes

Ingredients

- 1 cup frozen raspberries and blackberries
- 1 medium frozen banana, peeled
- 1 cup fresh sweet orange juice
- 1 cup baby spinach
- 1 tbsp hulled hemp seeds
- 1 tbsp unsweetened cocoa powder

Directions

Add all the ingredients to a blender and process on medium speed until smooth.

Pour the smoothie in to four glasses and enjoy immediately.

CONCLUSION

I believe now you understand how a plant-based diet lifestyle can be beneficial to you. I hope that the book answered all questions you may have heard about this style of dieting and that you can start to make it work for you. If you are still hesitant about entirely giving up animal products, you don't have to. The main take away here is that you make plant-based meals the main part of your diet as you make baby steps to transition into a full plant-based lifestyle. You will soon realize that your body and mind start to feel better, stronger and healthier. You can't fix your health until you fix your diet!

The book is conceptualized with the idea of offering you a comprehensive view of a plant-based diet and how it can benefit the body. You may find the shift sudden, especially if you are a die-hard fan of non-vegetarian items. But, you need not give up anything that you love. Eat everything in moderation.

You will love reading this book, as it helps you to understand how revolutionary a plant-based diet can be. It will help you to make informed decisions as you move toward greater change for greater good. What are you waiting for? Have you begun your journey on the path of the plant-based diet yet? If you haven't, do it now!

9 781914 176065